"From the President of the United States to a president of a small company to the president of the local garden club, this book is not only a 'must read,' it is a 'must use.'"

"In *Get Them on Your Side*, Sam Bacharach told us how to get people to rally around an idea. In *Keep Them on Your Side*, he's telling us how to manage for momentum, that is, how to make things happen. These two books have a wealth of knowledge, based on the experience of a first-rate academic mind. Bacharach has an unusual talent for translating ideas into the world of practitioners and for bringing the experiences of practitioners into the world of ideas."

"Bacharach's two books, *Get Them on Your Side* and now *Keep Them on Your Side*, are together the best works I have read on leadership. If you want to know how to put your ideas in place and manage for success, these are the books you need."

Tony Panos
President
Performance Training Inc.

"Organizations are littered with great ideas that never see the light of day because their sponsors were unable to navigate the realities associated with managing change. *Keep Them on Your Side* offers a pragmatic how-to for achieving success as skillful leaders move from concept to action."

Dave Pace
Executive Vice President, Partner Resources
Starbucks Coffee Company

"Sam Bacharach is a master of the ins and outs of organizational leadership. His books, *Get Them on Your Side* and now *Keep Them on Your Side*, provide a roadmap for those who wish to get ahead in any organizational setting."

Steve Cassidy
President, Uniformed Firefighters Association of New York

LEADING AND
MANAGING FOR MOMENTUM

KEEP
THEM
ON YOUR
SIDE

SAMUEL B. BACHARACH

Director of Cornell University's Institute for Workplace Studies
and author of *Get Them on Your Side*

**PLATINUM
PRESS™**

Avon, Massachusetts

Published by
Platinum Press™, an imprint of Adams Media,
an F+W Publications Company
57 Littlefield Street, Avon, MA 02322. U.S.A.
www.adamsmedia.com

Platinum Press™ is a trademark of F+W Publications, Inc.

ISBN 10: 1-59337-729-0
ISBN 13: 978-1-59337-729-8

Printed in the United States of America.

J I H G F E D C B A

Library of Congress Cataloging-in-Publication Data
Bacharach, Samuel B.
Keep them on your side / By Samuel B. Bacharach.
        p.   cm.
ISBN-13: 978-1-59337-729-8
ISBN-10: 1-59337-729-0
1. Organizational behavior. 2. Employee motivation. 3. Leadership.
4. Management. I. Title.
HD58.7.B3417 2005
658.4'092—dc22
2006019984

This book is available at quantity discounts for bulk purchases.
For information, please call 1-800-872-5627.

Contents

DEDICATION

For Ben and Yael . . . *
You are my momentum

Names appear in alphabetical order.
Both made equal contributions to my happiness.

Acknowledgments

The subject of this book is sustaining momentum and keeping people on your side. You have an idea. You want to fulfill it. To do so, you gather people around you and hope that they'll help you finish what you started. Because they're friends, they agree to come along for the ride and help. They form the type of supportive coalition that goes the distance. But, several months into the writing, when things aren't quite going well, when you don't know what to write, when the weather is lousy, you become bored, exhausted, and figure it's not worth the effort. Acquaintances and colleagues are sympathetic and tell you to put the project away and pick it up next semester or next year. Your friends are less sympathetic and tell you, "Get your act together and get this show on the road." That's the difference between friends and colleagues. Friends tell you the truth and go the distance with you, even when the project seems impossible. I have been blessed in this project by a wonderful group of talented, smart, and decent friends.

First, I would be remiss if I did not thank my undergraduate students at Cornell. Throughout the years they have taught me much. ILR (Cornell's School of Industrial and Labor Relations) undergraduates generally represent the best: smart, capable, and willing to be challenged. I'm especially grateful to all the students in my New York City internship program. Discussions with this small group of wonderful people have greatly enhanced this project. For the last eight years I've also been influenced by a great group of adult students at Ben Gurion University, where once or twice a year I retreat for a week or two to discuss my ideas with young practitioners. If they think they learned from me, great, but I have learned from them.

Ed Knappman and Jill Alexander believed in this project from the start. Ed has been wonderfully supportive of my writing in the last two years. Jill stuck her neck out, knowing that the rhythms and idiosyncrasies may make chaotic schedules and delayed deadlines. During the last phase of this project Kelly Lee Patterson, who just as I tired of getting examples, reminded me of some basics, like Mary Kay. My colleagues at the ILR School at Cornell University have always treated me with kindness and support. For over thirty years they've provided me with a home. In my effort to cross over from the world of elegant theory to the world of practical talk, Gary Fields, Harry Katz, David Lipsky, and Robert Smith were especially supportive. Stuart Basefsky, the genius of information gathering and an intellectual detective with an electronic magnifying glass, has been of help in immeasurable ways. Tony Panos and Tom Willett always made me think I had something to say to practitioners and acted as a sounding board for ideas. Gal Oron, Ilan Shapira, Joe Miccio, and Steve Cassidy—men who stand on the frontline—taught me more about workplace culture than any textbook. Stacia Murphy, a friend and a role model for twenty years, helped keep much of this in perspective. Stacia has always been there when I needed honest dialogue. Sara Edwards, who kept the graduate program in New York moving, showed the type of success and entrepreneurial effort that made the institutes I run look good, giving me time to play around with ideas. Sara brings to everything we do the shadow of perfection, intellectual ideals, and quality. Her voice has helped me stay on track. Adele Smithers-Fornaci and Christopher Smithers were, as always, in my corner. The Smithers family relationship with the Bacharach family means a lot to me.

Val McKinney proved to be a precise and thoughtful editor throughout this process. Scott Birch has been very helpful in bringing his graphic touch to my material. Michal Baron and Dana Vashdi both were extremely helpful at key points in the project and generous with ideas and time. Richard Singer, a consummate street-smart union politician and a fellow George Mossey fan, met me at the Cafeteria on 17th Street for breakfast and let me just groan. Amos Drory has been a good friend, providing me the opportunity to teach in the desert that I love with adult students and close to my family. He's also been more than a kind supporter.

Peter Bamberger, for many years now, has been my research partner. He is truly one of the best academics I've ever known. Without him, many of the projects of the last two decades would not have been possible. Most importantly, he has been a true friend.

My colleague for over thirty-five years, Ed Lawler, took time out from Pilates and art classes to have dinner at our favorite fish restaurant to work out ideas in a way that only he can. Ed, past dean of the ILR School, and one of the leading social psychologists in the world, is the type of scholar who brings rigor and insight into everything he does. A few hours with him beats all the academic brown-bag lunches in the world. Bill Sonnenstuhl got me into this mess in the first place by suggesting that I write two books and pointing me in a direction I never intended to go. But Bill didn't just drop it with the idea; he, being the friend and academic he is, stayed with me all the way. Bill is one of the best critics I've every met. He is insightful and to the point. I admire his intellect, and most importantly, I appreciate his empathetic under-standing and his friendship. Hilary Zelko came through as she always does, able to pinpoint the exact idea or particular concept that I missed. Hilary gave me some of the best advice I've ever gotten—write the way you speak. David Yantorno read the manuscript over and over and helped me visualize where it was going. The graphic work he did on this volume and the previous volume, as well as all his visual support, has made me a clearer thinker. David has impacted me in how I think. His graphic work, his sense of space, color, and form, has become part of my expressive vocabulary. David has given me the capacity to be an old guy who is comfortable with technology.

Four people have taught me special lessons about momentum. Stephanie Sutow is the type of person who stays in there even when in each corner there is a wall. By her sheer projection of decency, she will always have me on her side. This year Nick Salvatore taught me what it means to keep people on your side and to never give up. Derek Walcszek, who built a house for my family in the country, has shown the tenacity and creativity that changes dreams into reality, and vision into substance. Derek has shown me that you can go a long distance, even with disagreements, and still come out as friends. David Yantorno has taught me to keep it all in context and when necessary, to get up and keep on walking.

Yaacov Hefetz—what can I say? His artwork has helped me find a new expression. I would visualize what I wanted to say in pictorial form, and he would create it. He is a superb artist whose major work is found in numerous collections. We seem to work together as one mind. But why not? Our mothers were the best of friends beginning in 1925. So it's to be expected. His art has brought me joy for years.

Jim Biolos has worked with me for many years on a variety of projects and I cannot thank him enough. He gives, and gives generously. I come up with an idea, and Jim improves it immensely. I come up with a case, and Jim tells me what's wrong with it. I come up with a two-by-two, and he comes up with a three-by-three. His is truly a creative mind, able to work within and outside of the box. Many of the cases, illustrations, and ideas have been improved by his input. Indeed, some are his creation. Who else but Jim would come up with Martinez and micro-finance in Chapter 7? Or push me to think about the welfare state in the organization? Jim has taught this academic to lighten up. He helped me find my confidence. I've learned so much from Jim. I can only hope that he's gained as much from his relationship with me as I have from my relationship with him. And then there is history—Larry, Martin, and the Valley Stream Synagogue.

Katie Briggs. Katie Briggs!!! I began to work with Katie several years ago when she took a position at the institute I head. Her original position was administrative assistant. She is now budget director, seminar director, chief editor, research coordinator, project manager, tactical political adviser, and most importantly, the final authority on what is or is not garbage. Not one word is written here without her approval. She is truly a master of not simply the structure and grammar of the English language, but the tones and nuances of the English language. While I may be the king of clichés and jargon, she is the master of staying on theme. The hours upon hours that she has given to this project have been the most wonderful gift I've received throughout my years in academia. Without her support, without her good eye, without her stern hand, without her empathy, this project would not have been done. If I have good intentions, she is the momentum behind the good intentions. I owe her and her husband Matt much more than dinner at a Portuguese restaurant on Perry Street. Katie's support of this effort is testimony to the fact that late in life you can make a good friend even in the workplace.

And then, Ben and Yael. This book is important, but going to Brooklyn to watch my ten-year-old appear in an avant-garde theater, or seeing him play ball at Pier 40 or J. J. Walker, or going to the MoMA with him is wondrous. Yael, my wife, does more for me than I'm entitled. Before her, I was moving forward. Since being with her, I have momentum.

Because of all these friends, the wind is at my back and it's a beautiful morning. I think I'm going to get a cup of coffee on Bleecker Street and go with Ben to the Houston Street playground.

Introduction

Did you ever wonder why some projects never get off the ground? Why do some ideas never see the light of day? How come some visions just fizzle away?

It was a brilliant idea. It was what you needed to do, and poof! Before you knew what was going on, it just faded away. In the real world, things don't disappear because of magic. They disappear because no one took charge, no one took the lead, and no one displayed the managerial competence necessary to get results. The reality is that all too often visions and promises result in nothing. Success is about coming up with a viable agenda, getting people behind your initiative, and sustaining momentum so people will stay on your side and your ideas will be implemented.

Leadership books generally focus on this "vision thing" but they neglect the pragmatics of getting things done. They fail to let you know what steps you need to follow in order to be proactive and show results.

True leaders are proactive. They're able to get a critical mass of people and/or groups on their side *and* they are able to sustain momentum by keeping people on their side. They have both political and managerial competence. My last book, *Get Them on Your Side* (Platinum Press, 2005), shows how you can achieve political competence. Specifically, I show you how to identify allies and resistors, get people on your side, mobilize coalitions, and begin to roll out your agenda. This volume is a guide for keeping people on your side and sustaining momentum for your agenda. Specifically, I will address the managerial competencies that you need for putting your agenda in place and making things happen. I've found in my research that political and managerial competences are learned (and learnable) skills. If you are not very good at keeping people on your side, you can be. If you are not strong at implementing for results, you can be. There is no reason why you should *not* be a *proactive leader.* Developing proactive leaders was the inspiration for the last book and it is the inspiration for this book.

What is expected of a managerially competent leader? The bottom line is that managerially competent leaders not only come up with good ideas and create action, but also implement the ideas and sustain action. You can be charismatic. You can be charming. You can take as many courses in leadership, supervision, communication, finance, and marketing as you want, but your skill as a manager will be evaluated in terms of your ability to keep things going.

You can tell that all is not going well when you hear comments like, "Everything fell apart under her watch." Or, "Nothing got accomplished when he was at the helm."

And even, "She talks a good game, but that's about it." Failed managers cannot escape criticism regarding their inability to sustain momentum. Managerially competent leaders who sustain momentum are complimented at all levels of their organization with sentiments such as, "He really got things moving." And, "She promised a lot, but she really delivered." And, "He's not just talk; he shows results."

Sustaining momentum is the litmus test of managerial competence. Managerially competent leaders stay on top of the game, they stay one step ahead of their organization, their colleagues, their constituents, and their workers by anticipating obstacles, dilemmas, and uncertainties that may slow down or derail their agenda. The capacity to make sure that others will stay committed to an initiative and go the distance is the true test of managerial competence. A managerially competent leader leads and manages for momentum. He or she freely gives others the capacity to keep things going, to go the distance, to go the extra mile. Managerially competent leaders are able to sustain momentum under the worst of circumstances. They can take their projects all the way, keep people on their side, and go the distance.

Leaders who are managerially competent can go the distance because they understand there is more to momentum than the mythical "big mo." It is not just a locker-room cliché. It is a concept, a perspective that truly successful leaders know how to use. They know how to use it because they understand that the momentum—the big mo—is comprised of basic managerial skills.

If you are managerially competent you know how to vary your leadership style. You know when to be directive—to lay down the law and set expectations—and when to be facilitative—to listen, incorporate, and integrate. You know that sustaining momentum and keeping people on your side is a matter of walking a tightrope.

You understand the structural component of momentum. You know when and how to give people the resources and capacity they need to go all the way. You know that sometimes resources are not the answer and sometimes they are very much the answer. You understand the performance dimension of momentum. You know how and when to monitor performance and how to make corrections without stalling your initiative and creating inertia. You understand cultural momentum. You understand how to use culture as a tool for motivation and control. You understand political momentum and how to mobilize support and anticipate opposition.

The key to keeping people on your side is creating action—not getting stuck—and moving forward. This volume will specify what it is you need to do to avoid inertia, procrastination, bureaucratic bottlenecks, stall tactics, hesitation, and all the things that prevent you from rounding first base. This volume will help you become managerially competent so you can become a proactive leader who can sustain momentum and keep people on your side.

Chapter 1

You've Got Them on Your Side—
But Will They Go the Distance?

In many ways, Ellison was the right person to take over. The company conducted an exhaustive internal and external search and Ellison was consistently on the top of the list. His vision of moving into China and his idea of making serious headway in the service sector by expanding the consulting activity was what so many on the board hoped to achieve. His self-confidence and sense of calling enabled Ellison to mobilize the majority of board members. He was a great campaigner who left them dazzled. Eight months after he took the helm, however, doubts began to surface. Ellison, somehow, hadn't delivered. Maybe, just maybe, Ellison knew how to campaign, but didn't know how to get results. There were meetings upon meetings, and two sets of consultants, yet, nothing had moved along.

If you can't keep people on your side and the ball rolling, if you can't manage the pitfalls of inertia, you're no leader.

When you get rid of all the drama and all the rhetoric, when you distill all the hoopla down to nuts and bolts, what is leadership all about? It is about getting things done. If you can't get something done, your leadership is, at best, questionable. You can stand on a mountaintop and preach. You can paint the most beautiful visions of the future. If nothing gets done, does it really matter? Leadership is not simply about vision; it's about your capacity to be proactive and your ability to translate your vision into real results. Leadership is not simply about inspiration; it's about your capacity to translate your vision into a concrete agenda. Leadership is not simply about charisma. Leadership is about getting people on your side, sustaining momentum, and keeping them on your side. Leadership is about your ability to be proactive. Putting it simply, a visionary who is incapable of being proactive is a dreamer, not a leader.

In recent years, there's been an almost cultist obsession with the notion of vision, giving leadership a quasi-spiritual dimension, as though leadership were the capacity to see what has not yet been seen by others. As though there were one person per organization who could "see the future" and the organization was fortunate to have attracted this marvelous asset. Vision implies the use of inspiration and intuition, a sense of calling, a premonition of what needs to be done. Iconic leaders, like Clara Barton, Franklin D. Roosevelt, and Earl Graves, were indeed visionaries. But unlike passive "visionaries," they were not only people of vision, but also people of action. They were not just leaders; they were proactive leaders. Clara Barton recognized that in addition to needing medical attention, wounded Civil War soldiers were in dire need of medical supplies. She took action to solve this problem and eventually set up an organization (the American

Red Cross) that continues to help people around the world obtain medical supplies under life-threatening conditions. Franklin D. Roosevelt's New Deal also demonstrated how a vision could be translated, through action and implementation, into a series of initiatives that fundamentally changed the course of history. Earl Graves channeled his commitment to improving the economic well-being of the African-American community by establishing Earl G. Graves, Ltd. Acting to implement his vision, Graves founded *Black Enterprise* magazine in 1970 and continues to provide other products and services to improve the economic development of the African-American community. Today Graves is considered one of the country's most influential businesspeople. These leaders translated their vision into viable organizations that delivered real products and services. They were able to secure the help of others and to garner the necessary resources; they had the perseverance, commitment, and support to implement their ideas into organizations that sustained momentum and moved their vision ahead.

Indeed, how many "visionary" leaders who did not show results can you name? Not many. And if you can name them, it is more likely due to your disappointment with what they weren't able to accomplish, rather than for their vision. Although many aspire to be visionary and may even think of themselves as visionary, the reality is that truly successful visionaries are proactive, displaying both the *political competence* to mobilize people for action and the *managerial competence* necessary to sustain momentum and keep people on their side to achieve results. They take an inspiration and translate it into policies and organizations that can implement their ideas. Failed leaders are often those who come in with the grand ideas but who are incapable of translating those ideas into concrete results. Vision without accomplishment verges on hallucination.

When organizations seek leaders, they are immediately predisposed to look for inspirational leaders who have new ideas. How often have you heard of organizations recruiting a new leader and trusting that this one person will have a new idea that will redirect the organization onto a path of growth and prosperity? Frequently, visionary leaders are recruited with the expectation that they will see new ways to get things done, get people to think differently, and bring perspectives that others didn't see before. But new ideas aren't enough—and it is this notion that separates the true visionary leaders from the dreamers. It is, indeed, easier to enhance an organization's capacity to come up with good ideas than it is to enhance an organization's capacity to put those ideas in place.

It is easy to underestimate the difficulties that stand in the way of putting ideas in place. The tendency is to think that a good idea will carry the day; but it simply won't. On many occasions, individuals in organizations don't change their ways unless some crisis forces them to do so. Because interests are often entrenched, risk is often large, and routine well established, hesitation and resistance may be a stronger force than a good idea. Inertia is the name of the game. You may know where you want to go, but you may not know how to get others to join you in getting there. Vision may be seductive and charisma may be appealing, but these traits by themselves are not enough to create and sustain action in organizations.

Once you have the vision and direction, you must take action. You must take charge and actively execute.[1] You must become proactive. If the difference between visionaries and proactive leaders is the capacity to get things done—what turns a visionary into a proactive leader? What are the components of proactive leadership? First, proactive leaders have to have the political competence to mobilize people around their idea and get them on their side. Second, they have to have the managerial competence to sustain momentum, keep people on their side, and implement.

The Two Components of Proactive Leadership

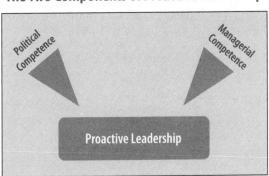

Political Competence

Managerial Competence

Proactive Leadership

Political Competence: Get Them on Your Side

Political competence is the ability to understand what you can and cannot control, know when to take action, anticipate who is going to resist your agenda, and determine whom you need on your side to push your agenda forward. Political competence is about knowing how to map the political terrain, get others on your side, and lead coalitions.[2] More often than not, political competence is not understood as a critical core competence needed by all leaders at all levels of an organization. All too often, it is the unstated competence. In organizations, we talk about everything but rarely do we admit that in order to get things moving, we have to be politically competent. If you get a successful leader to talk about how things get done in organizations, you may hear something like this:

Look, I knew if I didn't have Martha on my side early, I'd never get this idea rolling. She doesn't control a lot, but what she does control is critical. If I didn't get her onboard early, she and her staff would be in rebellion. The trick was to get Martha to buy-in early. After Martha was onboard, I could turn my attention to Hank in IT. Hank and his staff tend to be insular, and they are concerned with the nuts and bolts of security. But with Martha onboard, Hank would know that I could get the resources necessary to get this thing off the ground. I had a few casual meetings with Hank and then I met with him and most of his people. Next week, I figure I'll get Martha's people and Hank's people together, but tomorrow I have to make sure they are both on my side. The last thing I want to do is go into a meeting without their full public backing. This is a new idea, and if I don't launch it right without a full coalition behind it, it ain't going anyplace.

That's the voice of a proactive leader who is politically competent.

Politically competent leaders develop a compelling agenda. Few people are going to rally around your ideas just because they like you or because they feel they have to support you. The roots of long-term leadership are in having an idea or agenda that serves a real need in the organization, makes sense, and generates excitement among a solid base of constituents or stakeholders. The strongest agendas both raise awareness of key challenges or opportunities and lay out an approach to achieving desired results.

Once you have an agenda, you can go about the next important foundational stage: assessing your allies and resistors. In short, this is a process of political analysis. You are identifying the key stakeholders—internal and external to your organization—who have a stake in the outcome of your agenda and who probably have a position or strong opinion about your approach.[3] It is during this stage of the process that you will identify those who are clear allies, those who are likely to be strong resistors, and those who may swing either way. This may seem like a process of simply developing a list and checking it off, but it may involve a series of discussions with key stakeholders in order for you to really understand where they stand in relation to your agenda. You will find, coming out of this process, that there are those who may disagree with what you are trying to accomplish and/or those who disagree with how you propose to achieve those objectives.

With your political homework in hand, you then go through a process of gaining initial support for your agenda. This certainly includes securing key allies. But it may also involve doing things that keep your strong resistors at bay or that move potential allies a little closer to your camp. At this stage, you are looking for enough critical mass to take some initial action in pursuit of your agenda. That critical mass may be as few as two people or as many as a division. Critical mass is however many people are needed to get your agenda "off the dime."

With some support for your agenda, the next critical stage is getting real buy-in. This is the process of converting verbal support or conceptual support into real action. It is the not so subtle process of shifting some of the weight of your agenda from your shoulders and onto the shoulders of others. Getting buy-in is a process of negotiation, of demonstrating your credibility as a leader, and of convincing others that your agenda will result in real benefits to those who are active supporters.

Politically competent leaders are campaigners. They are great during the primaries; they build their base in Iowa, take it to New Hampshire, and close the deal in the South before they even get to the convention. They know how to draw in supporters and get support from constituents. They are great at getting things on the road. They can make you feel that success is right around the corner. All you need to do is join their coalition. At minimum, they will make you believe that you have much to gain by joining them and much to lose by ignoring them. To succeed in an organization, this is a skill that proactive leaders must have.

Once you proceed through this political process, you will have people on your side. You've built a foundation for your vision and agenda. You've established your beachhead, but that's all it is—just a beachhead, only a start. Now you have to implement your idea, sustain momentum, and keep them on your side.

Managerial Competence: Keep Them on Your Side

A lot of energy is spent on getting people behind an idea. Unfortunately, this is only one part of the story. Remember that candidate with the great ideas? How often have you realized that once in office, the candidate was incapable of making things happen? He didn't have what it takes to keep others on his side. In office, he floundered. The message was well articulated, but poorly executed. Sure, he had people on his side, but he couldn't keep them moving. He had everybody convinced to go along for the ride, but he just couldn't drive the bus. The key to managerial competence is your capacity to sustain momentum. Without it, your supporters will abandon you and you'll have fewer people on your side. Managerially competent leaders understand that by keeping the momentum going, they'll keep people on their side, and by keeping people on their side, they'll keep the momentum going.

The key to keeping them on your side is to give them the sense that things are moving along in a positive way, so they don't burn out, become disenchanted or alienated, and turn against your project. To do this you must make sure that the group doesn't stall, but has the capacity to move the project ahead. You want to make sure that they aren't caught in unnecessary bureaucratic bottlenecks. You want to make sure they don't choke with the anxiety of indecision. You want them to have the confidence and support they need to keep going. You want to make sure they don't get sidetracked by other agendas or pulled off target by competing goals. You want to make sure procrastination is minimized and inertia is overcome.

Long-term success is about keeping them on your side and going the distance. You have them in your corner; the challenge is how to sustain momentum. How do you keep things moving? How do you prevent people from getting stalled? How do you avoid getting pulled off target? How do you dodge the bottleneck? How do you guard against inertia? How do you keep away from the choke? How do you steer clear of procrastination? How do you conserve their energy to go the distance? These are the challenges of sustaining momentum. These are the challenges of managerial competence. Managerial competence is your ability to sustain momentum and make sure that your agenda is put in place while keeping people on your side.

While political competence is about your capacity to mobilize, energize, and coalesce people around your idea, managerial competence is about your ability to sustain the initiative, move toward a goal, and define who is going to do what, who is going to be accountable to whom, how people are going to be evaluated, how you're going to keep the group together until the mission is accomplished, and how you're going to deal with obstacles and challenges. Managerial competence is about your ability to sustain momentum and implement.

A proactive leader is managerially competent—consistently aware of the changing environment and aware that any organization is not unlike a raft moving down the river. At one point you may decide who will be on what oar, and who is responsible for what, but around the bend, a torrent of whitewater may mean that you have to change how you're going to get things done. Managerial competence implies your capacity to stay focused on the goal while adjusting resources and activities to deal with constantly emerging contingencies. If you're managerially competent, you have both close and distant vision—you have to be able to deal with minutia while looking ahead and being aware of what adjustments need to be made. While political competence is your ability to deal with strategy, managerial competence is your capacity to deal with daily logistics and tactics. Successful proactive leaders combine political and managerial competence.

If you are politically competent and not managerially competent, the results can be all over the map. You can mobilize people around an idea but you won't be able to implement the idea. You'll excite people about where you want to go, but you'll end up burning them out, alienating them, and your initiative will collapse.

You've Got to Have Both

Take Carly Fiorina and the merger of HP with Compaq. Fiorina was a highly successful executive. About three years after becoming CEO of Hewlett-Packard, she laid out an ambitious growth agenda for HP that included a merger with Compaq Computer. Fiorina used her strong selling skills and her political competence to build initial support for the proposed merger. In a heated proxy fight, Fiorina's agenda prevailed over Walter Hewlett's belief that "the company should expand through innovation and organic growth"[4] (Hewlett is the son of HP's cofounder). She was able to get shareholders, Wall Street analysts, and some key HP executives on her side.

From spring 2002 through spring 2005, Fiorina tried to implement the merger, sustain momentum, and deliver the expected growth results. But Fiorina ran into roadblocks. Although she was highly effective at getting people on her side for the boardroom fight with Hewlett, she was unable to keep them on her side.

The analysts who supported her—and the merger with Compaq—turned critical or, at best, neutral on the "New HP." Shareholders and the board were supportive early on, but their support waned quickly as the company's stock price and earnings stagnated. And employees—many of whom were skeptical about the merger in the first place—became cynics and never really seemed to get behind Fiorina's agenda. Although Fiorina built initial support for her agenda, over time, she was unable to keep them on her side. By 2005, Fiorina's support had become so fragmented that there was little she could do to shield herself from criticism and the eventual loss of confidence on the part of HP's board of directors.

Aside from Fiorina's inability to keep people on her side, she also had a problem implementing her agenda for results. Like many other mergers, the promises of the HP-Compaq merger were much easier to fulfill on paper than in the market. Fiorina had promised growth through innovation, through efficiencies, and through synergies gained with customer relationships. But three years into the merger, HP hadn't reduced its costs in the personal computer business; it had some new products (but no major innovation); and it hadn't yet realized the synergies of its combined customer relationships. Results were mixed throughout the company, and Fiorina's "vision" had neither the support nor the results she needed.

The combination of waning support and uneven implementation put up a devastating roadblock in Carly Fiorina's push to sustain momentum. By early 2005, the lack of momentum drove a loss of confidence in her ability to lead the combined company. In February 2005, Fiorina was asked to resign as CEO of HP. Although her first three years at the company had been marked with success and reasonably strong support, she was unable to sustain the momentum she needed to implement her new agenda.

It is not at all clear whether Fiorina lost her support because she was unable to show results or whether she was unable to show results because she lost support for her agenda. But the bottom line is clear: Fiorina was unable to sustain momentum at HP.

Fiorina is by no means the only talented leader who was unable to sustain momentum. Franz Xaver Ohnesorg's tenure as executive director of Carnegie Hall illustrates other problems that can emerge and prevent a leader from sustaining momentum.

Ohnesorg joined Carnegie Hall as executive and artistic director in September 1999. Ohnesorg's agenda was ambitious and an incredible challenge, given the culture and traditions of Carnegie Hall. Ohnesorg's agenda had three major thrusts: change the way performers were booked; open the hall to more contemporary music; and reduce the number of tenants in the studios above the hall.

Almost immediately after taking the reins, Ohnesorg showed his autocratic leadership style and commitment to delivering on his agenda. Just as early, his style began to ruffle the feathers of the Carnegie Hall staff. Ohnesorg was demanding, had high expectations, and a fair amount of pressure from the high-powered Carnegie Hall board to show results. He remained fixated on results.

After nearly one year at the helm, Ohnesorg was showing results. The plan to reduce the number of tenants in the studio space was being implemented and eviction proceedings were well under way. Ohnesorg leveraged his relationships with avant-garde composers and also brought star-studded performances onto Carnegie Hall's annual season roster. He moved the organization down an aggressive road toward developing a five-year plan and completing a $65 million recital hall. By most measures of strict results, Ohnesorg's two years at Carnegie Hall were productive indeed.

But results tell only half the story, if that. Ohnesorg's inability and seeming disinterest in building support among his organization members put him—and the organization—in a precarious position. Four senior staff members resigned during his first year. And an anonymous group of employees wrote letters criticizing his authoritarian style. Ohnesorg's approach and disregard for relationships with his staff created a furor that not only undermined his performance, but also left a cloud hanging over the reputation of the Hall itself.

By December of 2000, the tension finally came to a head. Ohnesorg resigned from his post and took on the position of executive director for the Berlin Philharmonic (where he lasted about a year). He received public praises from the chairman of the board and the president of Carnegie Hall. And he had results to show for it. But those results came at the expense of the continued momentum of the organization toward its goals and with the loss of some very talented senior people.

Ohnesorg was clearly a very competent individual. His credentials undoubtedly gained him instant credibility with the Carnegie Hall organization. And he certainly had the support of the board of directors early on. Regardless of talent, regardless of the results he produced, Ohnesorg's inability to keep people on his side led to a very fast, very public demise. In this sense, Ohnesorg's tenure at Carnegie Hall exemplifies the skills and shortcomings of the leader who tries to do too much without enough support from others.

Like Ohnesorg and Fiorina, if you take the helm in a new position, you can expect almost immediate criticism and some resistance. People will challenge your ideas and question your intent. The economy may change, making what was relevant yesterday no longer relevant today. The political landscape may shift, leaving you more vulnerable. You will have to make adjustments and corrections. You'll have to pull your team together, evaluate what you're doing, and develop a new plan. Furthermore, you may have to make adjustments in how you organize your program (or team) and what your expectations of each individual are. All of this may impact the commitment of all the people who were on your side when you first took the reins. Your challenge is to now sustain momentum, keep them on your side, and prove your managerial competence.

Frances Hesselbein is an example of an enduring leader who, for nearly twenty years, was able to sustain momentum for her ambitious agenda for the Girl Scouts of the USA. When Hesselbein was named executive director of the Girl Scouts of the USA in 1976, the organization was in very poor shape. The demographics of American girls had changed and the Girl

Scouts had failed to maintain its relevance with its primary constituents—young American girls. By the mid-seventies, ethnic minorities made up an increasing segment of the total population of American girls between the ages of six and fifteen. Yet, the percentage of these minority girls who were members of the Girl Scouts lagged well behind their actual numbers.

Although Hesselbein was with the Girl Scouts for twenty-five years before being named executive director, she was something of an unlikely candidate. She was not a Girl Scout when she was young and she didn't have any children of her own. In fact, she started in the organization as a volunteer troop leader in Johnstown, Pennsylvania, in the 1950s. Her original plan was to work with the troop for six weeks, until the Girl Scouts could find a permanent replacement. Eight years later, she was still the troop leader. Gradually, she took on increasingly broad administrative and managerial roles within the organization.

When Hesselbein became the head of the organization, she developed her agenda that was built around the core mission of the Girl Scouts: to help young American girls realize their high potential. The Girl Scouts strayed from this mission to a point where the organization seemed to be simply sustaining itself, rather than helping and developing its constituents.

One of the first items on Hesselbein's agenda was to change the structure of the organization. The Girl Scouts of the USA had become as highly centralized a bureaucracy as there was in the United States. Hesselbein knew firsthand how this structure inhibited the organization's ability to be creative, to serve its local troops, to become relevant once again, and to truly pursue the organization's mission.

One of her early initiatives was to restructure the organization from its strong, central hierarchy to a flat, networked organization model. Hesselbein described this design as "circular structure or circular management system"[5] because of its absence of a top-down hierarchy. In the organization structure, Hesselbein placed herself in the center of the wheel structure.

Under this new operating structure, volunteers and staff were responsible for acting in a manner consistent with, and in pursuit of, the core principles and values of the Girl Scouts of the USA. But these volunteers and staff made decisions that used to be made at the top. Rather than implementing programs from the top that may not have been relevant or engaging to a particular local troop, the local units had much greater latitude in shaping programs, activities, and initiating innovative changes.

Hesselbein felt this new structure would make the organization more adaptive to the demographic changes taking place in the United States. But, more importantly, Hesselbein felt that this more free-flowing structure would enable the organization to return to a focus on its core mission and values and enable local leaders to attract and serve the diverse groups of young girls who were the organization's target members.

An agenda like this was by no means simple to undertake. At the early stages, Hesselbein faced all the resistance, questioning, and challenges that come with any change effort.

Hesselbein was able to build support from the board of directors and from many regional and local Girl Scout chapter volunteers and staff. Hesselbein was, indeed, adept at "getting them on her side." And her tenure began at the height of the Equal Rights Amendment movement, *Ms. Magazine*, and a strong feminist-led movement toward giving women and girls a heightened sense of self, self-worth, and power.

Once Hesselbein established some momentum, sustaining this momentum was very challenging. Although her new structure distributed power, innovation, and decision-making to local members, the risk was that the organization would become fragmented, would lose a sense of membership commitment to a common mission, and could indeed become less effective than the organization Hesselbein had inherited. Hesselbein worked tirelessly to implement systems that fostered communication, idea exchange, and collaboration across local chapters. In addition, she practiced what she preached: that the most important thing about the Girl Scouts of the USA organization was its mission, values, and core principles. This theme was continually communicated and reinforced from the "center" on out to the rest of the organization. Hesselbein felt that if local chapters understood and actively pursued the mission, they would make effective decisions. As Hesselbein often says, "Leadership is a matter of how to be, not how to do it."[6]

From 1976 through 1990, Hesselbein led the Girl Scouts of the USA. Peter Drucker called the organization under her leadership one of the best managed in the world.[7] In presenting her with the Presidential Medal of Freedom, President Clinton remarked that "she reinvigorated the organization with her commitment to inclusiveness and to upholding the Girl Scout mission of empowering each Scout to reach her highest potential. Under her guidance, the number of minority Girl Scouts tripled and overall membership soared."[8] Frances Hesselbein demonstrated the capacities, actions, and attitude that it takes to sustain long-term momentum in an organization—to keep people on her side and to implement for results.

The fourth example is the case of Jeff Bezos. When Bezos founded Amazon.com in the early 1990s, it was with a visionary agenda to change the way bookselling was done. Bezos spent the first few years clarifying his agenda and getting people on his side. He was remarkably adept at doing so and benefited from a venture investment environment that was predisposed to putting money and influence behind an Internet venture. With the wildly successful public offering of Amazon stock in 1997, Bezos had demonstrated his capacity, much like Fiorina and Ohnesorg, to create momentum. At that point his challenge shifted to whether he could sustain the momentum.

Through the end of the 1990s, Bezos's agenda had been largely successful. Amazon's share price had skyrocketed. The online bookseller had made a clear dent in the industry, and its brand recognition among consumers was unparalleled in the online world. Bezos was a widely regarded genius who was actually able to make things happen. During this time, Bezos expanded his original agenda of online bookselling to become more like an online department store, offering a wide range of products and services using the Amazon.com shopping and shipping technology and infrastructure. The one significant thorn in his side was that the company was still not profitable.

When the Internet bubble burst in 2000, Bezos came under much deeper scrutiny. Over the course of the next year and a half, Amazon's stock price plummeted. Critics and analysts stepped up the pressure for Amazon to show a profit, and Barnes and Noble and others made profitable growth much more difficult for Amazon. The momentum Bezos had created was seriously threatened across a number of fronts.

But Bezos was able to sustain some momentum by showing Amazon's first quarterly profit at the end of 2001. Not only did this give his leadership at least a temporary "stay" among analysts, shareholders, and critics, but it also enabled Bezos to consolidate his support internally and to demonstrate that their efforts were beginning to pay off.

Amazon's expansion efforts continued to pay off in 2002. The company showed its first annual operating profit; it deepened the degree of personalization of its site; and it greatly expanded its partnerships and product offerings. Amazon's stock price began a two-year ascent and, once again, Bezos was able to demonstrate an ability to initiate and implement for results and to keep people on his side, in support of his agenda. And even though Amazon's stock price slipped again in 2004–2005, Bezos had built sufficient momentum and political currency to keep the company focused and moving forward on its agenda.

As this book is written, Amazon faces a new breed of competition. Google threatens part of Amazon's bookselling franchise. Regardless how Bezos handles this latest threat to his leadership and to the company's performance, there is no doubt that he has been able to demonstrate a unique ability to build and sustain momentum for his agenda over the long term.

From these stories of success and failure comes an obvious, but often underestimated, tenet: Effective proactive leadership is a combination of getting people on your side, sustaining momentum, and keeping them on your side. It is about having the political competence to generate interest and support for your agenda. And it is about having the managerial competence to keep people engaged and to deliver results. You must have both. If you are only politically competent but cannot follow through on your vision and agenda, you will end up as the "nice guy who couldn't get anything done." If you are politically competent but not managerially competent, you may get some things accomplished in the early stages, but your efforts may be undermined by others or unwind quickly because of your inability to maintain support and sustain momentum.

The key to your managerial competence is keeping them on your side. And the key to keeping them on your side is to sustain momentum. If you sustain momentum, truly implement, and achieve, others will definitely stay in your corner.

Chapter 2

Demystifying Momentum

At a corporate retreat in Tahiti, the CEO stands up, and in his charismatic style, addresses the assembled managers about the importance of the "big mo." The big mo is part of the company's culture. It's a can-do organization. The CEO pounds in phrases like, "We got to win with the big mo," "Remember, never lose momentum," and "Keep the wind at our back, smooth sailing ahead." Everyone leaves Tahiti with the motivation to get something done. Jack, a plant manager from Nebraska, feels inspired, if not moved, by the call to sustain momentum. But, as Jack's plane gets closer to Omaha—and farther from Tahiti—reality sets in. For Jack, the CEO's push for the "big mo" dwindles into diffuse inspiration rather than a concrete strategy. He realizes he has to translate the euphoric "big mo" of the Tahiti meeting into practical little mo's that will work in Omaha.

You've been in the dumps about the Chicago Cubs all season long, but now you're glued to your TV screen. They are on a six-game winning streak. The announcer maintains that late in the season the Cubs have established momentum. The coach has them in the right mindset. He has the right players on the team. He knows what needs to be done and how to do it. The team is pumped up and ready to go the distance. Now the trick is to keep the momentum going. In our culture, momentum is often used in the context of teams, as in a sports team. A team that has momentum is one that's on the move. It's a team that's charging ahead. It's a team with a sense of inevitability. It's a team that can only be stopped through real effort. A team that has a lot of momentum is not going to be stopped easily. The question is—what turned this team around? What has given this team a full head of steam? What does it mean to say they hit their stride? What does it mean that they have momentum?

The concept of momentum is ingrained into our daily life. Sports teams rally to "keep momentum going . . . " or they carelessly "let momentum slip away." In the financial pages, you can read about "new evidence of momentum for economy . . . " or reconsider your stock purchases when you see that "momentum wanes as the Dow falls. . . . " But it is political life where momentum is most evident. Momentum on the campaign trail gives the candidate and his staffers a boost and improves his standing in the media, and, one hopes, his standing in the polls and at the ballot box. One presidential contender declared, "My campaign has great momentum and great energy." His challenger, on receiving a bit of good news, said, "I think that's going to give me the momentum to move forward." The loss of momentum is cause for concern and regret. A politician whose party is losing support before a primary tells the press, "If we had the momentum, we'd still be in the game."

❧

"The project lost momentum. That is the long and short of it."

"We had it in our hands. There was no way that I thought they could get to market before us. We had the people, the direction, but somehow, it just slipped away. We shouldn't have gotten sidetracked—adding that one function cost us too much time, too many resources. We took our eye off the ball and let it slip away."

"It didn't take much, did it? It's amazing how quickly they caught up and passed us. After that, we just lost it. We never got back in the game. I guess we'll have to remobilize around a different product. I hope the R & D team is up for it. I don't know how many more times we can go to the well with them."

You've probably heard or said something to this effect about some aspect of your organization in the past year. And *momentum* is one of those words that upon hearing, everyone shakes their head with understanding—but understanding it in more of an amorphous sense, rather than a definite one.

Momentum is something of value, and something to aspire to, and it is something that can quickly be taken away by forces beyond one's control. A meeting of the Federal Reserve ("the Fed") can stop stock momentum. A hot pitcher on the other team can stop the Cubs' winning streak. A contender can suck the momentum out of a frontrunner's campaign. To sustain momentum requires focus and vigilance.

When momentum describes a group on the move, the analogy is drawn from physics, where momentum is defined as "mass in motion." The textbook definition of momentum is that everything has mass. So, if an object is moving, then it has momentum—it has mass in motion. There are two variables that define an object's momentum—mass and velocity. The physics lesson ends with an equation: The momentum of an object is equal to the mass of the object times its velocity, or momentum = mass × velocity. The object's momentum is precisely proportional to the object's mass and velocity. In a social context, mass means that you want people on your side. The more people on your side, the greater your potential for long-term success. Velocity means you want them to remain active and to focus on what needs to be done. Managerially competent leaders who want to sustain momentum are challenged to keep people on their side and keep them active.

Consider again the political candidate. The more people he gets on his side, the greater the mass. The more people believe in his ideas, the greater his potential momentum. If, on top of that, he can instill a sense of belief, a sense of commitment, a sense that together they can accomplish anything, he will maximize velocity. Therefore, a politically competent leader who has successfully mobilized people and got them on his side will begin with immense momentum, which will allow him to drive his ideas to victory. The problem with the world in which we live is that it abhors a vacuum. Inevitably, there is resistance. Momentum has to be sustained, because at any point, the massive support that you have gained because of your political competence may abandon you, and the velocity of your initiative may face obstacles and slow you down. They may be on your side in the beginning, full of optimism and confidence, and active in your campaign. If you don't focus on sustaining momentum, your campaign may be brought to a halt by burnout, exhaustion, resistance, and indifference.

While your political competence may allow you to start with a lot of momentum, dealing with obstacles will challenge your capacity to sustain momentum. Successful organizations, successful departments are those that sustain momentum. The basic challenge to your managerial competence is your capacity to manage for momentum—that is, your capacity to keep your projects, your initiative, and your people moving ahead in spite of emerging obstacles and uncertainties. But it isn't easy to answer questions like, "How can you keep my group moving?" Or, "How can I make sure there's follow-through?" Many leaders believe that momentum is simply an ability to keep busy and to keep making progress toward one's goals—that it's a one-dimensional concept that is either "on" or "off." This couldn't be further from the case.

Beyond the Big Mo

Often momentum is regarded as a monolithic and mystical "big mo." How many times have I sat in Yankee stadium, watching the home team lose games, but by August, the wind is at their back and they seem to have caught the "big mo"?

From the stands, it seems that suddenly all the stars aligned and they're back in the groove. But is it as mystical as all that? Is momentum all that monolithic? All that mystical? Or is it, in fact, that away from the limelight, in practice, and in the locker room, Joe Torre is capable of leading and managing for momentum? Managerially competent leaders understand that in order to control the big mo, they need to manage the four dimensions of momentum so their initiative stays on track, stays on people's radar, and remains something that the organization continues to support.

The first dimension of momentum is *structural momentum*. Leaders who emphasize structural momentum are likely to believe that keeping things moving is a function of giving people resources and making clear who does what. Embedded here is a logistical notion: If you want to sustain momentum— worry about resources and responsibility. The second dimension of momentum is *performance momentum*, with emphasis on achievement and evaluation. If you want to sustain things in an organization and keep things moving, you need to make sure that evaluations are conducted, progress is measured, and feedback is given. The third dimension of momentum is *cultural momentum*. Leaders who sustain momentum place an emphasis on the group culture, where the cohesiveness of the culture and social psychological mechanisms, like peer pressure, will sustain projects to completion. The fourth dimension of momentum is *political momentum*, where leaders make sure that conflict is dealt with and that opposition is either challenged or incorporated.

When you view momentum in this way, you can develop a sense that there is something you can do to sustain it. That it isn't simply this high concept that football games are made of. How you manage for momentum will depend on how you allocate resources, how you make corrections, how you maintain commitment, and how you deal with criticism. Proactive leaders do not view momentum as an unquantified state over which they have no control. Proactive leaders see momentum as a multidimensional commodity that can and must be managed in order to ensure the success of their initiative.

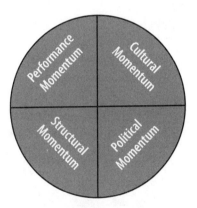

**The Four Dimensions
of Momentum**

Each dimension of momentum is important in its own way to the success of your project. Each is different, but each is critical. Sometimes you have to place your attention on one and not the other. Sometimes you need to balance them all. Sometimes you simply decide to float. No matter what the demands of your particular situation are, the key to sustaining momentum is constant focusing and adjusting. Managerially competent leaders who are able to see their project to completion are constantly aware of what they have to do in order to move their project ahead. Is it a question of resources and responsibility (structural momentum)? Is it a question of not evaluating performance accurately or often enough (performance momentum)? Are the beliefs of the group a problem (cultural momentum)? Or maybe it's a problem of old-fashioned sabotage (political momentum)?

Maintain, Monitor, Motivate, and Mobilize for Momentum

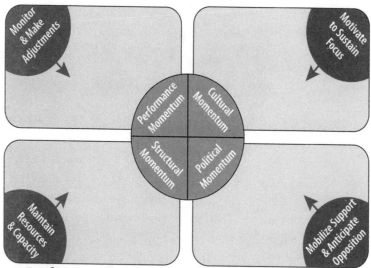

By focusing on sustaining momentum in each dimension, you significantly improve the likelihood that your initiative will continue to have wide support and remain vital. Each of these dimensions of momentum requires you to apply a different component of managerial competence. To keep structural momentum going, you will need to *maintain* resources and capacity. To sustain performance momentum, you will need to *monitor* performance. To maintain cultural momentum, you will need to *motivate* others. And to keep political momentum going, you will need to *mobilize* support.

Structural Momentum: Maintain Resources and Capacity

Often, when trying to keep things moving, leaders fail in their managerial competence by not giving people the capacity to keep moving. You are ready to put your initiative in place. You have your political base of support. The first thing you need to consider is—what resources are necessary, who will do what, and how will they do it? Managerial competence demands that you understand what others need in order to get their job done. If you don't empower your people with the basic capacity to get the job done, all the cheerleading in the world, all the visions will come to nothing.

Consider the following quotes for a second. What's the message? "Sure I know what they want to get accomplished, but it seems to me that they're not making any resource commitment. The other day I asked them for another administrative assistant. I have a project that I'm ready to roll out, but they're playing it so close to the vest; they're telling me that they want me to use the secretarial pool. How can I use the word-processing pool when I need someone who can not only type, but also deal with the crazy constituents we have out there? The other thing is, if we are not allowed to turn the systems over to the Macs for the design capacity, I don't know what we're going to do. We have a lot of young people who are more familiar with them and need them for our projects."

Maybe this is familiar: "I understand they want to break up the departments into teams. I understand that they believe smaller teams give more punch for the buck, and they think they'll be able to turn things around quicker—but who on earth is responsible for what? Do I report to the department chair? Do I report to the regional people? Who do my people report to? It's not clear to me that these functional teams can be coordinated. It certainly isn't clear to me where the buck stops. It may be great for momentum, but I'm not sure who's in charge. We're going to need some accountability."

Have you heard this: "For years we've each had some degree of say regarding how we deal with individual clients. My strength and the strength of my team is that we know our territory, know who we're dealing with, and know how to fine-tune our sales pitch to our particular market. I mean, we're in the service business and now they want to come out with a manual that dictates language and protocol. I understand they believe that routinizing the presentations will allow us to move things quickly and save time, but I'm not sure that will work in our market. It's a huge shift. I think we're going to need more flexibility than they're offering."

Suppose you're going to put in place a new Human Resources Information System (HRIS). Everyone agrees that it's a good idea. But as a managerially competent leader your first responsibility is to make sure your team has the basic capacity to implement the agenda. Capacity means giving people the appropriate resources, appropriate roles, and appropriate activities that will allow them to implement. Sustaining structural momentum deals with this fundamental issue of capacity. If people don't have the right resources, if they aren't sure what they are and are not responsible for, if they don't know how much autonomy they have in their job, they will constantly be bottlenecked and slowed down.

Managerially competent leaders who sustain structural momentum are experts at allocating resources and empowering individuals and groups to perform specific tasks or processes in the pursuit of their agenda. The most effective leaders understand that their ability to keep the support of others and move their agenda forward is tightly linked to their ability to deliver results and to engage others with the responsibility and authority for getting things done.

When you think of resources, you think of something very simple—those very basic things that are needed to engage in the work at hand. Organizational theorists often talk about these things as the "instruments of transformation"—the hammers, the equipment, the people that allow you to get your product or service out. Generally, there are two types of resources: human resources and inanimate resources. Human resources are generally thought about as support services. For example, teachers often require the assistance of teachers' aides as well as that of other teachers, physicians require the assistance of nurses and those in the allied health professions, and managerial staff often require the assistance of administrative staff and external consultants. In some cases, this may not involve employees who are in direct contact with the position under study, but rather systems that regulate the services humans provide (e.g., word-processing pool) or units that provide temporary and often indirect support services (e.g., an online computer help desk).[9]

Inanimate resources are obvious. We sometimes spend so much time speculating about motivation, leadership, and inspiration that we forget the basic lesson that if you give a farmer a hoe he is going to move a lot slower than if you give him a tractor and a combine. If you give a teacher a classroom with a whiteboard and without computers, it will be more difficult to implement that new interactive math program that is part of the state's agenda. Equipment may be viewed as the physical and tangible items employed in the performance of job responsibilities. Equipment refers not only to the physical apparatus used in the direct processing of job-related materials and information, but also to the peripheral factors often required for the proper use of these apparatus (e.g., lighting, electricity, fuel, etc.). Thus, for a teacher, equipment includes not only the whiteboard but also the textbooks that provide the primary source of information to be presented. For a chemist, equipment not only refers to the apparatus in the laboratory, but also to substances used in experiments and the lighting required to view the results.[10]

At first appearance, the issue of the allocation of human and inanimate resources as discussed here seems somewhat obvious: Give a man a hammer so he can build a house; give a doctor the support of an experienced surgical nurse so she can operate. But it's not that simple. Failed visionaries are often those who forget to think on this most basic level. To succeed, you really must have a good understanding of what resources people need to get the job done. Achieving this understanding is often more difficult than you would think. Consider the example of Abraham Lincoln and George McClellan. In 1861, shortly after Lincoln gave General McClellan command of the army of the Potomac, McClellan faced a much smaller army in Virginia. Lincoln kept pushing McClellan to take action, but McClellan kept coming back, maintaining he needed more troops and more equipment, arguing that the army of Northern Virginia was larger than the president and the other generals thought. Lincoln understood that the moment was right and felt that McClellan had more than enough troops and equipment. McClellan felt he wasn't ready. As he wrote to his wife, "I do not intend to be sacrificed."[11]

Resource allocation is not as simple as it appears. Your estimate of the resources needed to maintain momentum may not match the estimates of others. The McClellan incident is a lesson to the leader who wants to sustain momentum. When have enough resources been allocated? When is there a genuine lack of resources? When is the supposed lack of resources just an excuse for not doing one's job?

In building capacity, you need to have a broader notion of resources than just human and inanimate resources. You have to give people the right support staff and right equipment if you want to sustain momentum. But you can also tie people up by not making it clear to them who is responsible for what. The second aspect of structural momentum is how you're going to design the power (reporting) relationships, the communication relationships that will occur among the key actors. How often have you seen instances where people have the resources, but somehow, they don't know who is accountable to whom, who has final authority, and with whom they should communicate? How often have you seen organizational projects flounder because no one knew who was really in charge? If you want to sustain momentum it is important that the organizational structure makes it clear to everyone what the lines of authority and responsibility are.

Continuing the story of Lincoln and McClellan, Lincoln never made it clear to his general that the final authority belonged to him, the president. Lincoln did not assert his role as commander in chief. Furthermore, McClellan dismissed Lincoln's, as well as Secretary of War Stanton's, appeal for action as the meddling of civilians in military affairs.

Everyone needs to know where the buck stops. Traditionally, this has meant making a choice between a hierarchical model, which is bureaucratic in nature, and a flatter, less bureaucratic organization. Hierarchies allow you to achieve

a high level of accountability and organization. If you believe
the momentum is best sustained by coordination and accountability, you should seriously consider making the chain of
command clear to everyone. You should make sure that individuals know with whom they have to coordinate, to whom
they report, and who really is in charge. When you think of
this type of structure, you think of a traditional setting like
public sector bureaucracies, factories, and the military, where
the primary emphasis is on the process of implementation. At
any given moment, everyone knows who is in charge.

In the last twenty years, there has been a greater emphasis
on flatter organizations, where the reporting structure is
more ambiguous, coordination is more subtle, and where
communication is more open-ended. This approach is based
on the assumption that what's important is for people to work
together as teams. The boundaries are not easily definable.
Communication networks are constantly changing. Even
who's in charge may vary from project to project. The attrac-
tion of such an approach is that it allows people to act in a
dynamic, collective way. The downside is that sometimes
you get caught in interpersonal micropolitics of who really is
in charge, which makes it almost impossible to move ahead.
The challenge for you in sustaining people's capacity is not
only to give them the right resources, but at the same time, to
give them a clear understanding of how authority and responsibility are defined. On certain occasions it may be important
to define it in a hierarchical manner and other times, in a
flatter manner. In the management literature, this is known

as the organizational design issue. How do you set up your project in such a way that it has the appropriate authority structure?[12]

As you try to sustain momentum for your agenda, you will inevitably face the challenge of making the work highly predictable and repetitive so as to maximize efficiency, while trying to keep workers engaged and enthusiastically supportive of your agenda. You need to consider carefully how you will approach the work processes by which your agenda is being implemented.

In building capacity, a managerially competent leader has to consider how to define the work of individuals. Are you going to sustain momentum by defining the work in a routine manner, so it becomes a series of tasks? Or will you sustain momentum by making sure that most people operate as problem solvers rather than executers of specific tasks? This is known as the job design problem. How do you design the jobs in such a way that momentum is sustained?[13] Do you simplify them or do you enrich them? Again, the issue here is one of balance.

For example, should teachers teach according to a set curriculum that specifies each hour's activity, or should they show some variation in the classroom? How much autonomy should workers have? Should they be encouraged to find new ways of solving problems or should they solve problems by following protocol? What kind of training or professional development do your people need to execute? What do you need to do to further develop their skills for long-term success?

In maintaining capacity for structural momentum, managerially competent leaders must deal with resource allocation, accountability, and work processes.

Performance Momentum: Monitor and Make Adjustments

You've established structural momentum. You know who is going to do what. You know who is responsible for whom. You know how you'd like things done. You've shown your managerial competence in giving people the capacity to execute. However, having done this isn't sufficient. As things move along, you have to be able to make corrections and adjustments to ensure that momentum is sustained. One of the keys to your managerial competence is your capacity to keep things moving in the intended direction. You may have organized everything in the way you think it should operate, you may have decided who does what and when, who makes what decisions, but if you don't stay on top of it, if you don't correct and make adjustments, you'll find that your project just gets bogged down.

Sustaining momentum requires monitoring performance and making corrections along the line. You need to constantly ask yourself, "How are we doing?" and then make people decisions that ensure that answer is, "We're on track." You need to frequently assess the people on your team, discuss their performance, and make changes as needed.

It is not enough to ensure that your group maintains the capacity to get the work done. You must make sure that they use that capacity and live up to its potential. Performance momentum is sustained by your capacity to monitor what is being done.

It is in this domain that so many leaders fail to sustain momentum. They may have built capacity, organized their efforts well, and got the right people onboard. And then, strangely enough, they just walk away. They walk away because it is uncomfortable and difficult to monitor people and projects. All sorts of issues arise. When to monitor? How often to do it? Who will you evaluate? What kind of criteria and standards will you use? Then there is fear that with monitoring you will inhibit momentum.

Have you ever said to yourself, "If I evaluate them now, it will just slow them down. They'll spend so much time considering what I said, they'll just back down. What if it makes everyone around here paranoid and they resent my remarks? Maybe I should keep it a loose dialogue rather than a focused, pointed evaluation. Maybe I should drop it for now. We're not really in crisis."

Any leader who has embarked on monitoring performance to sustain performance momentum knows that this can be the most time-consuming aspect of their leadership role. Not only does it require the time to understand and assess people's performance, but you also need to spend a substantial amount of time documenting that assessment in some way and then having the conversations with each person in your organization to build shared understanding and agree on a plan for improvement and development. A minority of leaders do this well—which is why when someone in your organization does do it well, it is usually noticed.

As Lincoln understood, he had to stay on top of McClellan. This is obvious from the numerous visits that Lincoln made to McClellan's headquarters in Washington and in the field. While many have interpreted McClellan's failure to take action as being a function of his narrow professional vision, stubbornness, and resentment of civilian intervention, the problem could have very well been with Lincoln. Lincoln's low-key manner, his sensitivity to McClellan as a person, his fear of offending a general, upon whom he was so dependent, may have made him reluctant to evaluate McClellan fully. Maybe Lincoln failed to be as direct as he should have been. Maybe he spoke in generalities rather than specifics. Maybe he wasn't clear about the criteria McClellan would need to fulfill. Maybe he should have invited McClellan to the White House instead of going out to the field to meet him. Maybe Lincoln gave too much deference to McClellan's uniform and professional expertise, which prevented Lincoln from dealing with McClellan's shortcomings in a timely manner. Lincoln's obfuscation allowed McClellan to delay, procrastinate, and, ultimately, avoid action.

As an initiative moves forward, you need to do more than just sit back and hope that momentum will carry the day. Even with talented people who do not need much direction, you still need to monitor their performance and provide them with feedback on how they are doing. You need to take an active role in their professional development and communicate with them in a way that helps them remain engaged in your agenda and eager to do more, learn more, and to improve their performance, as needed. JetBlue's David Neeleman understands that the success of his company depends on his ability to monitor every detail. He directly involves himself by getting on his own carriers, speaking to his people, listening, and suggesting ways in which corrections can be made. He understands that if JetBlue is to sustain momentum, it is his responsibility to make sure that necessary corrections are made quickly throughout the organization. Neeleman is an exception. Too many leaders fail this basic test of managerial competence and distance themselves from the monitoring process.[14]

When you effectively monitor performance, you are accomplishing two important objectives. First, and most obvious, you are paying close attention to the progress your initiative is making against its goals. By doing this, you can spot opportunities for improvement early on and cut off any surprising shortcomings down the road. Second, and, perhaps, more important, you are demonstrating concern for the people who are delivering on your agenda. When you evaluate performance and have the kind of dialogue that helps others understand your expectations, understand how you feel they are doing, and how they can improve and develop professionally, you send a very strong message to your organization's members: What they do matters and that you remain interested in both your agenda and in their development. As such, great monitors like Neeleman also have to be great mentors.

They don't just evaluate what needs to be corrected but give guidance, often through example, on how such corrections can be put in place. Performance momentum requires leaders to mentor as well as monitor performance.

Cultural Momentum: Motivate to Sustain Focus

Why is it that in certain university departments academics keep on publishing, keep on producing, keep on working with their students many years, sometime decades, after they've received tenure? Why is it that in other departments the drop off in productivity is more dramatic? Sure, they publish and work with students until they receive tenure, and some may even continue working hard for a while, but they somehow slow down. The momentum isn't there; they lose focus. Some would make the argument that this has to do with resources, that in certain universities faculty are more amply rewarded and supported and are able to continue working on research and publishing papers. Others say that it is not a question of resources, but a question of sanctioning and monitoring—that the administration, department heads, and deans are not staying on top of the faculty. The third possibility, and the most likely, is that in some places publication—and continued publication—is not only rewarded, but is part of the professional and organizational ethos, part of the culture of working in the academic setting. In some departments, the focused drive of professors to continue to publish, the continued momentum, appears to come from what appears to be on the surface, self-motivation. In reality, however, it is the very culture that defines them as academics. Cultural momentum has to do with those psychological attitudes, beliefs, and cognitions that enhance one's sense of motivation and identity.

Motivation is about people's willingness to expend effort to achieve a goal. Are you motivated by rational calculation— "I'll do what's expected of me as long as I'm paid for it"? Or are you motivated by your status and reputation in the organiza- tion—"They are not paying me much anymore, but for me, continuing to write papers is what being a Cornell professor is all about"? Clearly, my colleague identifies with more than just himself and his own self-interest. His identity is wrapped up with the organization he works for and his profession. He has a sense that he is not just one alienated being, working in the factory. Rather, he is part of the communal organization and group culture that drives him to keep the momentum going forward.

Cultural momentum deals with the sense of collective, the social and psychological sense of purpose and belonging. Culture deals with the issue of keeping people together—the spirit of "we-ness."[15] For momentum to be sustained, it is not enough that you give people the structure and capacity to deal with uncertainty. It is not enough that you give them the resources, systems, and knowledge to keep going. It is not enough to make adjustments and corrections as you go along.

You also have to keep them socially and psychologically motivated, sustained, and directed.

Momentum is sustained by a leader's capacity to motivate, focus, and socialize individuals so they can feel like they're part of a group. By enabling others to engage with one another—and to feel part of a larger whole—leaders can sustain their agendas to completion and build commitment and confidence when the road becomes rocky. This is the role of cultural momentum and the leaders who are able to sustain it know how to motivate the group—that is, they reinforce the group's purpose, direction, and identity.

Have you heard, "We have a can-do culture"? Or, "We have a culture that stays on top of things"? Sometimes momentum is a question of your ability to ingrain the culture of the group into the individual. In some organizations, you walk in and you immediately have the sense that they can run with the ball and go the distance. Such a culture is one of "drive." Consider firefighters. Theirs is a culture full of tradition. They reinforce expected behavior through the stories of the heroic deeds of their brethren, by recounting pivotal events, important people and their actions. They tell and retell stories that subtly and not so subtly communicate how a firefighter is supposed to engage with the organization and build a sense of belonging among its members. Firefighters take action and extraordinary risk because of their strong sense of mission. As a result, their focused drive saves lives.[16] The most effective leaders of firefighters are able to sustain momentum by using the firefighter culture to inspire and deliver outstanding commitment and superior performance.

Imagine two groups with comparable resources. One group shows results, while the other can't seem to get anything done. They start a lot of projects, but they finish nothing. They don't have the capacity to go the distance. Sure, they may listen to the same CEO give the same call to action. But when it comes to implementing an agenda or demonstrating superior results, even though the teams have similar talent, a similar organization, "the B team," somehow falls short. Their agenda goes unfulfilled. You've seen plenty of examples of this. The new product launch, which was so highly touted, turns into a money pit. The reorganization that was supposed to improve customer satisfaction results in customer confusion. The rollout of a performance management system gets stuck in meeting paralysis. The best-laid plans become some of the worst-laid eggs.

In many of these cases, the X factor is cultural momentum. Using value and purpose, the leader of the "A team" created a sense of belonging, commitment, and collaboration among the group's members. People relate to others in the group. They relate to the group as a whole. In a real sense, they define themselves in relation to the group and/or the initiative. This is the foundation of cultural momentum that will get this team through adversity.

The leader of the "B team" is unable to build that sense of belonging and relatedness. On this "team," people largely feel like individuals who happen to be clustered together, but they don't have any deep feeling of belonging. When the agenda hits a bump in the road, members begin to question things. They point fingers. They criticize. They don't rally together. This team will lose momentum quickly. And the source of the leak is the absence of a cohesive culture.

Steve Jobs is one of the great motivators and sustainers of cultural momentum. When he founded Apple, he built a culture of innovative thinking and a sense of belonging in the coalition battling "the dark side" of the PC industry. Apple's early success was certainly due to its innovative design and its elegant and easy operating system. Its success was also due to Jobs's ability to sustain cultural momentum—to maintain that sense of belonging to the "Apple cause" and to keep on battling even though Microsoft and IBM were becoming the industry standard.

Fast-forward to 1997. Jobs returned to Apple and re-infused the cultural momentum that the company lost under John Sculley, Mike Spindler, and Gilbert Amelio. One of his first moves was to launch the iMac line of computers. It was, arguably, Jobs's ability to sustain Apple's cultural momentum that got Jobs and the organization through hard times from 2000 to 2003 and to remain focused on its innovative capacities with the introduction of the iPod music player in 2001. By 2004, the iPod had reinvented Apple and had helped drive up Apple's stock price fivefold. And through both his tenures, Jobs demonstrated the capacity to sustain Apple's cultural momentum—to create and nurture "believers" in Apple's products, its innovative capacity, and its commitment to "think different."

When trying to sustain cultural momentum, you need to motivate your team. You have to constantly make people believe and accept the purpose and direction of your efforts. The managerially competent leader understands that a group's culture should be strong enough to sustain commitment and identity, but not so strong that it creates an all-encompassing cult of enmeshed zombies. In sustaining cultural momentum you want to create an integrative, collective culture, but you do not want to destroy the capacity of people to reflect, deviate, and come up with creative alternatives.

Political Momentum: Mobilize Support and Anticipate Opposition

Often, the most obvious obstacles to sustaining momentum are conflict and criticism. There are always naysayers. There are always those who initially may have thought you had a good idea, but now openly question whether you are doing things the right way. There is always the potential of emerging countercoalitions that will challenge your direction. Maintaining momentum often tests your political instincts. When do you bring people onboard? When do you face the resistors? When do you ignore them? When do you dismiss them? The challenge is to know when to mobilize support and when to anticipate opposition. Leaders capable of sustaining political momentum understand exactly whom they should mobilize and whom they should exclude. They know exactly how much room to give people to criticize and discuss, but they never give them enough leeway to revolt.

President Lincoln faced many challenges during his presidency; one was dealing with Secretary of Treasury Salmon B. Chase. As treasurer, he was a valuable member of the cabinet, and he tirelessly raised funds for the Union Army. But Chase harbored presidential ambitions, ambitions of which Lincoln was fully aware. Lincoln did not work against Chase or his supporters. The president always treated Chase with fairness and kindness, and was not the least reluctant to appoint Chase supporters to key positions. Lincoln's close allies questioned Lincoln's political moves—preferring that the president keep the man who would challenge him for his job at arm's length. To explain why he treated Chase the way he did, Lincoln told a story about when he was a boy plowing a Kentucky field with a horse. The horse, which had been trundling along, perked up and practically ran to the length of the furrow. Lincoln noticed a chin-fly that had latched itself to the horse's hide. The young Lincoln's first inclination was to knock the fly from the horse, but his friend said it was a mistake, because it was the fly that made the horse work so efficiently. Lincoln remarked that if Chase "has a presidential chin-fly biting him, I'm not going to knock him off, if it will only make his department go."[17]

Lincoln understood that he needed Chase not as a follower, but as a partner, and partnership does have its costs. Lincoln understood that Chase's success as Secretary of Treasury was fueled by his ambition for the presidency. Lincoln saw himself as the chin-fly driving Chase, and indeed, would tolerate criticism as long as Chase was raising the badly needed funds for the Union Army and as long as Chase's countercoalition did not pose a serious threat to the president. One of Lincoln's major skills was his capacity to monitor Chase's internal opposition and sustain political momentum.

It's easy to dismiss leaders who are focused on political momentum as either Machiavellian or paranoid. The truth is that both of these descriptions ignore the simple reality that, at times, you have to be aware of unrest, you have to deal with hesitation, and you have to understand sabotage. Mobilizing people means making sure that you keep them on your side. You keep their interests focused and you make it clear that their early buy-in to your agenda will be rewarded with success. Mobilizers are constantly negotiating, constantly influencing, and constantly persuading.

Michael Eisner's tenure at Disney serves as an example of a leader who was highly effective at sustaining political momentum. When Eisner became the CEO of Disney in 1984, he was an "outsider" responsible for infusing fresh ideas and a focus on results to the struggling icon of animated film. Eisner developed his agenda for Disney—to build on the organization's core animation capabilities and to create a much more powerful film production business that moved well beyond cartoons and animated film.

Eisner quickly began to turn the company around and demonstrate results. Disney's stock price rose from about $2 per share (split adjusted) when Eisner took over to a high of nearly $45 per share in early 2000. Despite the success of Disney's stock, Eisner faced persistent criticism from within the organization and from around the industry. Eisner was a savvy monitor who was keenly aware of his critics and camps of resistance and who responded to those detractors with a range of strategies: from bringing them onboard with his agenda to moving them out of the company.

When Eisner joined Disney, he brought with him Jeffrey Katzenberg and Frank Wells. The three continued to bring on colleagues and professionals from the film business, helping Eisner build political momentum for his agenda. From 1984 to 1994, Disney's strong performance—along with his firm alliance with Katzenberg, Wells, and their staffs—enabled Eisner to squelch any resistance to his agenda. When Frank Wells died in a tragic helicopter accident in 1994, in addition to losing an effective operating officer and close friend, Eisner lost an important political ally.

From 1994 to 2003, Eisner began to face an increasing amount of resistance and opposition—particularly after his very public falling out with Jeffrey Katzenberg and the subsequent departure of other key executives. Despite the increasing opposition, Eisner was able to sustain political momentum. Sometimes that was through replacing executives. Other times it was through acquisitions and alliances with other organizations (e.g., purchasing ABC/Capital Cities, ESPN, and Miramax). Even when Disney fell on hard times from 2001 to 2003, Eisner continued to maintain his political momentum—with Disney's board of directors, with employees, and with industry analysts, vendors, and competitors. He used an autocratic style, bolstered by superior stock performance, to push his agenda through the organization.

By 2003, however, resistance to Eisner's agenda had grown to the point where Eisner was no longer able to maintain his political momentum. Whereas in the past Eisner had been able to use the company's performance as a way of overcoming resistors, now the company's poor performance fueled his opposition. In 2005, Eisner reluctantly stepped down as CEO of Disney.

Critics suggest that Eisner was a very poor politician. He alienated his closest people and was unable to build a management team that could provide the company with a long-term succession of leadership. Perhaps all of this was true. Yet despite expectations that Disney would turn to an outsider to replace Eisner, it was eventually Bob Iger, an insider backed by Eisner, who was chosen to become chief executive. Many in the company and the media perceived this as a political victory for Eisner.[18]

Political momentum is not always about being well liked and being a "model citizen." It is about your ability to mobilize support for and to deflect resistance to your agenda. In this context, Eisner will never receive any awards for being the most well-liked leader. Nor will he go down in history as one of the great people managers. What Eisner did remarkably well, however, was to build political momentum and then sustain this political momentum for his agenda over the course of twenty years. His political momentum was closely tied to the company's financial performance and to the degree to which others viewed him as a "genius." Eisner used both of those factors to sustain political momentum over his twenty-year tenure. But once those two sources of credibility eroded, Eisner's autocratic style undermined his leadership and stalled any momentum he had built for his agenda.

The challenge to your managerial competence is to be able to sustain all four dimensions of momentum. You want to keep structural momentum going by maintaining resources and capacity. You want to sustain performance momentum by monitoring performance and adjusting. You want to keep cultural momentum going by motivating others. You want to sustain political momentum by mobilizing support. It would be nice if the world were linear, where you could first maintain, then monitor, then motivate, then mobilize. But it's not that simple. Your managerial competence will be tested by your ability to be cognizant of all four dimensions of momentum along the way. Proactive leaders, who are truly managerially competent, know when to put emphasis on one type of momentum over another. Your managerial competence will be tested by your ability to continually maintain, monitor, motivate, and mobilize for momentum. Proactive leaders know that momentum is the key to keeping people on their side.

Chapter 3

Balancing Leadership for Momentum

We need a new coach. Basketball is just not totally predictable. You've got to give them some room to think. A little looseness in the game is what it is all about. You can't anticipate everything. This coach is confusing mentoring with monitoring. He is too ate-up with the game. The game is becoming too regimented for our guys. Everything is a drill. Everything is an exercise. He calls in all the plays. The team has absolutely no discretion. Sure, he runs a tight ship, but look what happened to our guys; the moment they came up against St. Luke's they got their ass kicked. St. Luke's plays a spontaneous game—run and shoot, shoot and run. The moment our guys came up against that kind of freestyle, they couldn't readjust their zone quickly enough. They're great at carrying things out, but they need to be a little looser. We need a little balance here!

Sustaining momentum is not easy. It requires making strategic choices, having the ability to understand contingencies and constraints, and most important, having the capacity to vary your leadership style. The foundation of your managerial competence centers on your understanding the subtleties of momentum. A managerially competent leader understands that sustaining structural momentum, performance momentum, cultural momentum, or political momentum involves making strategic choices.

In dealing with each dimension of momentum, you have a choice. When maintaining resources and capacity in order to enhance structural momentum, the challenge is whether to place an emphasis on *control* or *empowerment*. Controlling resources implies giving your team exactly what you think they need and defining their work and responsibilities in a specific, routine way. Empowerment means that you will give your team constant, flexible access to resources as well as a great deal of autonomy in conducting their daily activities. Structural momentum is sustained by managers who know when it is important to engage in control and when it's important to empower. Structural momentum is sustained by your ability to look at the contingent situations and decide which of these two styles is most appropriate. For example, during stable market conditions you may decide that centralized control is the best way to ensure that production continues at a constant pace. During a more turbulent period, with either rapid growth or unpredictable competition, empowerment may be more appropriate, giving people the capacity to make rapid decisions. The strategy for sustaining structural momentum is not absolute, but contingent.

When monitoring performance in order to enhance performance momentum a managerially competent leader understands when to put the emphasis on *evaluation* or *development*. Emphasizing evaluation implies checking performance and holding people accountable to the bottom line. It means you are clear and specific about standards and expectations. Development, on the other hand, is about your capacity not simply to "hold people accountable" but to "bring people along." It's about how you make sure that individuals constantly develop the skills, talent, and disposition they need in order to do what is necessary. Emphasizing development implies heavy use of feedback, dialogue, and training. While evaluation is about your capacity to keep things in check, development is about your capacity to mentor. These categories are not mutually exclusive. You have to consider when one is more appropriate than the other.

When motivating people with purpose and values in order to enhance cultural momentum the managerially competent leader can either try to *direct* people toward specific goals or try to *guide* their self-motivation. When you direct toward specific goals, you lay out the objectives, specify expectations, and sustain the culture by keeping the organization's members on point. When sustaining culture through guiding self-motivation, your focus will be on internalizing their self-drive and giving them a sense that they are an integral part of a coordinated team. Again, choices have to be made. While it may not be one or the other, under different conditions there are different ways to sustain cultural momentum.

When mobilizing support to enhance political momentum, a managerially competent leader *anticipates* conflict and *incorporates* opposition. You can accept that conflict is inevitable or you can show a basic concern with incorporating everyone on your team in order to reduce conflict. You can have your antennas up and be on guard, constantly worrying about where resistance and conflict will come from, or you can be at the other extreme, constantly integrating others into your mission. Again, you have to make a choice. If you are constantly on the watch for opposition, you may fall victim to a disabling mode of paranoid leadership. On the other hand, if you incorporate everyone, your naiveté may result in consensus building that goes nowhere. Sustaining political momentum is about knowing whom to exclude and whom to include. It's about anticipation and incorporation. It's about your capacity to keep people mobilized.

When dealing with each dimension of momentum, you have to know which leadership style is most appropriate: directive or facilitative?

Directive vs. Facilitative Leadership

The manager who relies on directive leadership takes a full-steam-ahead and do-it-by-the-numbers approach to momentum. Stick with the program, follow instructions, and implement. Tell them what you want, how to do it, and when you want it done. The directive leader views the average person as not self-motivated, comfortable with inertia, and willing to avoid any possibility of chaos or uncertainty at any cost. Embedded here is the notion that in order to sustain momentum, people cannot simply be motivated, but that they must be driven, coordinated, directed, supervised, and pointed toward the organizational objectives. They must be given the means and the ends for pursing a task.[19]

In this context, momentum is best sustained by telling people what to do, controlling how they do it, giving them the resources to do it, and scrutinizing to make sure it happens. The emphasis is on the need for accountability, predictability, and routinization. The more you can predict events and make the activities routine, the greater your capacity to implement and keep moving. In social science, this is known as dealing with the anomie problem;[20] simply put, what people fear most and will slow things down most dramatically is the lack of direction, specifics, and norms. This means you want to make sure things are done right and quickly. You want to make sure people are not confused. You need to make everything clear. Directive managers believe that you maximize momentum by minimizing uncertainty and ensure implementation by maximizing control. Such managers take charge at the get-go.

If you choose to lead your group with a more directive approach, you probably believe that the environment in which you are operating is relatively stable and/or predictable or that responsiveness or flexibility need not be the organization's highest priority. Within this context, you want your group to have explicit, specific, clearly stated goals that everyone in the group works toward. You believe it is management's role to direct and labor's role to execute, and have no problem with power that is hierarchical and narrowly distributed. While the directive approach has fallen out of favor over the past decade, the economic downturn between 2000 and 2003 created an environment where leaders found it necessary and appropriate to be more directive in their approach and in their management systems.

Consider the New York City public school system and the changes that Chancellor Joel Klein, under Mayor Michael Bloomberg, introduced. The Department of Education operated with a fairly facilitative approach for decades. When Klein became chancellor, he ordered an overhaul of the public education system. For those schools that were not among the 200 top performers, he implemented a required curriculum and a new organizational structure to carry out the mandate of improving the test scores and quality of education. The New York City public school system shifted its emphasis from agility to control, from a facilitative management style to a directive management style.

Supporters of this directive management style think that it is critical to specify teachers' work activity and assume the work processes of teachers can be delineated with a required curriculum. Some would go as far as to create detailed job descriptions for teachers, and perhaps move toward a teacher-free curriculum. This style of school management emphasizes formal, hierarchical evaluations, a culture of bureaucratic accountability, and a minimization of criticism.

How does this directive approach address the special-needs student or the late bloomer? How does this directive approach work with the reality that teachers have multiple and nonpredictable problems to solve day-in and day-out? In a highly directed educational system, it is assumed that student achievement is primary and measurable. This, of course, assumes that all students are alike, that all teachers are alike, that solutions are clear, that the world is stable, and that a school can be run in an assembly-line fashion.

One problem with the directive leadership perspective as a way of sustaining momentum and keeping things going is the "what-if" scenario: What if things fail to go according to plan and no one adjusts or changes the plan? There are obviously certain problems with the full-steam-ahead mentality. It is one thing to steam ahead when the waters are still. It is quite another thing to do it on the rough seas.

Sometimes in order to sustain momentum you have to give people the capacity to initiate on their own. What do you want one of your staff to do when an unexpected problem arises in trying to carry out a new program and no one is around to consult? Do you want her to drop everything to make a phone call to New York for approval? What do you want your HR person to do when he is trying to convince colleagues in Minneapolis that while the new policy has some kinks, it can be uniquely adapted with some adjustments and fine-tuning in Omaha? Sometimes one second—that moment when someone is looking in their field manual, checking with you, or getting clearance—is enough to kill the momentum you already have. Sometimes there is no time to blink in spite of the uncertainty. In just such an instance you want others to act within parameters but also to show initiative.

In this context, it is not enough that people know the policy and steps of implementation they have to take. They also have to have the confidence to act quickly and with the assurance that you, as their boss, and the organization stand behind them. To sustain momentum it is not enough to have a directive plan of action; there also has to be a developed capacity to make adjustments—the capacity to come up against obstacles and maneuver around them. Therefore, you cannot sustain momentum by simply being directive; you have to be facilitative when the situation calls for it.

A facilitative leader puts the emphasis on an individual's ability to reflect,[21] innovate, and problem solve. When you are acting as a facilitative leader, you're aware that your role is to enhance people's capacity to make creative and appropriate decisions when faced with uncertainty. You want people to feel confident in their ability to adjust the plan in such a way that they won't be trapped in inertia, or put in place a radical variation of your intention that is no longer recognizable to you. A manager who places emphasis on facilitative skills to sustain momentum assumes that most individuals are self-motivated and appreciate challenge. They are willing to take risks and value being problem solvers. Therefore, they are unafraid of uncertainty and chaos. This perspective maintains that given the proper conditions, people learn, adapt, use their imagination, and live up to their intellectual potential.

Contrast the New York City public school educational approach with that of a Montessori school. A Montessori school educational approach is much more facilitative. Its emphasis is on developing a core set of values and "approaches to learning," as opposed to a typical public school's emphasis on having students learn specific facts and certain required skills. Sure, Montessori administrators and educators expect their students to have certain core capabilities and knowledge that a public school graduate would have. But they also believe that their approach will provide students with additional and important capabilities that may not be well developed through the more directive, public school approach.

Think about the issues you would face if you were an educator in a Montessori environment. Can you really predict with accuracy how specific students will progress? Perhaps you can in very broad strokes, but certainly not in detail. Can you reasonably set goals that are anything but broad? Probably not, particularly since you don't administer formal test scores. Can your work processes be made routine? Not really, given the variable nature of the curriculum and educational approach. You can see how the issues associated with a facilitative approach need to be very different from those associated with a directive approach.

This is not to suggest that Montessori schools offer superior education. Montessori learning was designed for a particular educational philosophy and to achieve specific educational goals. Therefore, the Montessori organization may attract teachers and staff who may be different than those attracted to working in the New York City public school system. This is a useful, although broad, way to contrast the philosophies, systems, and assumptions of the Montessori system with that of a more traditional public school system. As a leader or an educator in a school system, you need to understand the range of approaches and directions toward change. Your challenge is to move your system in a direction that can accomplish your objectives and that can accommodate the range of uncertainties that you face. In the case of the New York City public schools, Michael Bloomberg, Joel Klein, and key constituents clearly felt that the needs of New York City children warranted a more directive educational system, rather than a facilitative approach embodied in the Montessori example.

The manager who relies on facilitative leadership believes that the best way to sustain momentum is to maximize spontaneity and/or adaptability. Or, you may not actually believe that, but you understand that you cannot easily predict the future direction of your initiative and you need to be prepared to respond quickly. When times call for fast reaction and adaptability, leaders want to be more facilitative in their approach.

Consider Procter & Gamble's responses to uncertainty in its markets, technologies, and politics.[22] First John Pepper, and more recently A. G. Lafley, understood that fundamental changes in the business and the environment required a much greater emphasis on innovation and new products. P&G executives responded to the challenge by running its new product development and innovation efforts with a facilitative approach. Building on the successes of Procter's Corporate New Ventures (CNV) unit, the company gradually expanded this "looser" approach to innovation across the organization. This approach may not have worked in every Procter unit, but P&G's track record of successful new products over the past decade would not likely have been possible if it had been managed with a highly directive approach.

For a facilitative leader, organizations are more like networks than hierarchies; in these "learning organizations," workers are team members and problem solvers. Compared to the unilateral do-as-you-are-told directive leadership model, the facilitative leadership model relies more on connections among group members. Facilitative leaders make use of both formal and informal exchange, rather than top-down authority. Unlike directive leaders, who assume that only small groups have power, facilitative leaders distribute power more broadly (although the power is generally not distributed equally or evenly).

While a facilitative approach accommodates fast-moving, fast-changing situations, it can ignore some basic realities of implementation. Namely, implementation takes time and focus. While it is great to be nimble and responsive, when things need to get done, there needs to be some sense of efficiencies, clarity, and focus. Facilitative leaders often are unable to implement effectively and can fall on the knife of what's "visionary." In the pursuit of the new and the responsive, emerging leaders thumb their noses at the discipline and real work of creating routine, controlled systems, and measurement.

How can you sustain momentum when the assumptions of a facilitative approach meet the challenge of stable, low-growth markets? Suddenly, goals need clarity. Work processes need to be more directed. Power often needs to be consolidated. Each of these pressures challenges the facilitative organization.

Facilitative leaders address the uncertain realities of the modern work environment, where the real aims of the organization can be ambiguous and are continuously changing and where multiple aims are likely to be simultaneously pursued. Facilitative leaders ride a wave of unpredictable and shifting alliances, making them able to respond to change quickly. Make too many adjustments, however, and you'll find yourself either off course or in the doldrums. Make too many adjustments, you'll stifle momentum and find no one in your corner. Facilitative leaders may keep things moving but may easily find themselves sidetracked, and in need of a touch of directive leadership. Directive leaders will stay on course and implement the plan, but if they don't show the facilitative capacity for making adjustments, they may still fail in fulfilling the larger objective. In order to sustain momentum, you have to know when to be directive and when to be facilitative.

For nearly fifteen years Diane Keller rose steadily through the ranks of Specialty Beverages, a well-established *Fortune* 1000 consumer products company. The company was in the premium bottled water business and had made several successful acquisitions to diversify the company's activities and drive its stock price up by 30 percent over a two-year period. Specialty was a darling of the industry, not only because of the long-term growth of its stock price, but also because of its attractive product line of vitamin-enhanced beverages.

Diane had started at Specialty, just out of business school, as an assistant product manager. Over the course of her career at Specialty, she had taken on greater responsibilities. She had managed the development and launch of their very successful iced tea business and then had moved up to category manager for all hydration products. After eight years with the company, she was named chief sales officer. She was promoted because the CEO and the board felt that company sales were in the doldrums—they were not getting the market share they needed in both domestic and international markets. Every effort seemed to sputter and fail.

What the company needed was someone who could lead for momentum. Diane Keller appeared to be that person. She took charge immediately. She divided sales into seven regions: three domestic and four international. She centralized the fiscal function at the Chicago office. No longer would each section have its own budget, which would be examined yearly. When she took the helm, she decreed that all budgetary decisions were to be made at the Chicago headquarters. Each region had to adhere to the specific sales plan laid out by the central office. In fact, under her leadership, sales plans were defined for each field rep and sales scenarios were scripted, with reps being videotaped and coached. Evaluations were conducted every six months to make sure that each region and every rep met their targets. She defined the goals and reinforced them by establishing a culture of accountability. "You will be held accountable for your numbers," was her mantra. When it came to conflict and opposition, her attitude was simple: If you didn't follow the company line, you weren't part of the team. She was a classic example of a directive leader who maintained structural momentum by controlling what people did and the resources they were given. She maintained performance momentum by constantly monitoring to ensure performance. There could never be too many evaluations for Diane Keller. She sustained cultural momentum by directing people, motivating them by making clear her purpose and goals. Finally, she sustained political momentum by anticipating resistance, teasing out splinter groups.

Keller decided to take a position with CitogenPharma, a start-up biotech firm. Keller's mandate was to grow Citogen—to increase sales to take the company from its early stage to high growth. Keller was very excited by the challenge. After so many years at Specialty, she really needed a fresh challenge in a different industry. She also didn't want to be typecast as a "bottled water person."

Keller understood that success at Citogen was going to depend on her ability to sustain momentum. After fifteen years at Specialty she had come to believe the best way was through directive leadership. As quickly as she got on the job, she imposed the very model that worked so well at Specialty—centralized structure, constant evaluations, specified goals, and constantly anticipating opposition. She came to

Citogen with the same no-nonsense, stay-on-top-of-the-game attitude that kept things going at Specialty. However, Citogen was run in a very different way from Specialty and soon people were talking of leaving, burnout set in, inertia took over, and momentum, at best, was slowing down. In a young biotech firm, directive leadership was not going to sustain the momentum needed for success.

Citogen's leadership team was much younger than that of Specialty and many of the executives had little management experience. This was an organization that operated "on the fly" and had a staff committed to putting out fires and coming up with new ways of doing things. Diane thought this would be a refreshing challenge and an opportunity to infuse some of her more disciplined work style into this inexperienced company.

Diane was in the position less than six months when John Harding, Citogen's CEO, called her into his office for a meeting. "Diane, we need to talk. I am getting a lot of complaints about you. Initially, I thought it was just that you were a new, senior person, but now I get the sense that there may be a mismatch in your style with the Citogen approach. I know you're trying to move things ahead, but I think the problem is how you're going about it."

"I think I understand what you are saying, John. But I'm not sure I agree. You brought me in to grow this company's sales. I've run sales in much larger companies than this and I know the kind of systems and approach needed. Citogen's been very successful as a start-up, but the sales staff is all over the place. They do whatever they want, and they're wasting resources; they're one big happy family going nowhere. They need to be a little more regimented and systematic in their work."

"I agree, Diane. But people think you are a dictator. Listen, I hired you because of your deep experience. And I know that I alone cannot get us to where we want to go. But I need to sustain this organization's momentum and right now, your approach is threatening to stall our progress."

"What are you suggesting, John?"

"I'm suggesting breathing room. Let them keep some of their autonomy. Give them back some of their budgets. Lighten up a little on the evaluation. Have a little sense for the positive aspect of their groupness. Don't worry so much about their opposition. Get them involved. I know you're into direction, but try to be a little more flexible and facilitative in the way you manage. Do that and they'll go the distance."

"I'm trying, John. But it isn't easy for me. And I will continue to try to find that balance that you need. Just know that I think we both have the same goals in mind."

"I believe we do."

Diane spent the next several months trying to accommodate the quirks of Citogen and tried to be more flexible in how she operated. It wasn't particularly easy. The staff had developed a view of her as a "dictator" and weren't ready to dismiss that perception. And Diane was still not confident in her ability to be so flexible. She felt she knew what needed to be done. In her view, the staff was out of control. But she desperately didn't want to fail. This was her opportunity to prove to herself that she could be successful in more than one organization, which was something she wanted to show to her former colleagues. So, she worked hard to modify her approach, while trying to keep Citogen on its high-growth trajectory.

Balanced Leadership

In sustaining momentum in any arena, the challenge is how to balance directive leadership and facilitative leadership. Managing for momentum is a study of contradictions. It is a question of knowing how to balance these two distinct styles. Sustaining momentum demands the skills of a juggler and talent of a tightrope walker. Directive leadership sustains momentum through control, based on telling people what needs to be done, allocating resources, making expectations clear, defining goals, and establishing the parameters of success and failure. Facilitative leadership sustains momentum by creating a sense of community and a sense of autonomy. It is based on your ability to get people involved and to move members of your group to go one step beyond.

When keeping things going, managerially competent leaders define to what degree they want flexible, agile group members and to what degree they need people to follow "marching orders" to execute the agenda. During lean and difficult times, you may want to explicitly define the goals assuming that you believe that the more you delineate a goal the more you can control resource expenditures. During times of growth and resource abundance you may want to define the goals more broadly so that the organization is open to all available opportunities.

Day in, day out, managerially competent leaders choose management approaches that range from highly directive to highly facilitative approaches in order to sustain momentum, depending on the situation at hand. Your challenge is to know which way to lean.

Lewis and Clark: Balancing Directive and Facilitative Leadership[23]

You can probably think of numerous organizations that sustained momentum and where leaders proved their managerial competence by being sensitive to each of the four dimensions discussed above. When you think of sustaining momentum, consider the organizational challenges that Lewis and Clark faced when exploring the Louisiana Purchase. Lewis and Clark maintained structural momentum by controlling and empowering. They sustained performance momentum by monitoring—evaluating and developing. They kept cultural momentum going by motivating others—directing and guiding them. Finally, they sustained political momentum by mobilizing—anticipating and incorporating. Lewis and Clark understood that if they were going to keep things going and keep people in their corner, they needed to balance directive and facilitative leadership. This was the genius of their managerial competence.

Thomas Jefferson charged his good friend and personal secretary Meriwether Lewis to lead the first military exploration of the West. In Jefferson's opinion:

> *It was impossible to find a character, who to a complete science in botany, natural history, mineralogy and astronomy, joined the firmness of constitution and character, prudence, habits adapted to the woods, and a familiarity with the Indian manners and character, requisite for this undertaking. All the latter qualifications Capt. Lewis has.*[24]

Lewis, with his knowledge of politics, geography, and botany, possessed the technical knowledge and diplomatic skills to lead the expedition. While he had army experience, he lacked the organizational skills that would be necessary to carry on a lengthy expedition with a wide mission. Lewis understood that in order to keep people on his side and sustain momentum during a long and perilous journey he would have to balance his leadership style. Lewis's appointment of William Clark as his co-commander was a testament to his managerial competence and good judgment. Clark exemplified the traits that Lewis did not have himself, or lacked to some degree. Lewis possessed the technical knowledge and diplomatic skills to lead an expedition through unknown territory. But he clearly lacked the organizational skills and, perhaps, the hands-on experience of leading an expedition into the frontier. William Clark had both. As a rising military leader, Clark had a track record of successfully leading troops and overseeing the logistics of large-scale military projects. Clark was a lifelong frontiersman and extremely comfortable exploring new wilderness. In addition, he was an accomplished cartographer, and he had a profound knowledge of Native Americans. The combination of Lewis's scientific background, strategic sensibility, and frontier orientation with Clark's tactical ability would contribute to the success of the expedition.

Structural Momentum

Under the leadership of Lewis and Clark, the expedition was able to recruit highly skilled individuals who could not only handle the group's basic survival needs, but also were specialists in one of the key capacities the organization needed. Without an emphasis on building the right organization early on, it is unlikely that the expedition would have achieved its goals at a relatively low cost.

In maintaining the capacity of the expedition, Lewis and Clark emphasized control of resources. They allocated and controlled resources through a very structured hierarchy. The men felt that the best way to organize for a highly uncertain, dangerous expedition was through a very clear hierarchy of command. The three major divisions within the Lewis and Clark organization were hunters, boatmen, and interpreters.

To realize Lewis's agenda of finding a route to the Pacific Ocean, his organization was going to have to do three things well: hunt animals, both for food and for trade; navigate the sometimes treacherous river waters en route to the Ocean; and communicate and build relations with diverse Native American tribes.

Given the dangerous nature of the expedition, Lewis and Clark maintained tight control over the work processes. Traveling through an unknown wilderness, with many hostile strangers and changeable weather conditions, Lewis and Clark believed that directive daily work assignments were paramount. According to the diaries kept by members of the Corps of Discovery, the co-commanders made the distribution of work clear—everyone understood who would do what. Whether the task was to bring items from base camp back to St. Louis for delivery to Thomas Jefferson or to launch an exploratory mission to a Native American camp, roles and responsibilities were clearly laid out.

Performance Momentum

In monitoring to ensure performance, Lewis and Clark understood how to balance evaluation and development. Although Lewis and Clark brought on highly skilled, experienced people, they were extremely effective at developing people, and assessing and monitoring performance. Lewis and Clark set out their performance expectations and evaluation system early in the journey. Within the first few months of the two-year expedition, they court-martialed three men: one for desertion, one for "mutinous behavior," and one for sleeping on guard duty. These three disciplinary actions helped to define the leaders' performance expectations and sent a clear message to the rest of the corps. After these first three months, the only disciplinary actions taken were relatively minor.

In addition to discouraging unproductive behavior, Lewis and Clark implemented an informal system of rewards to recognize and encourage positive contributions. Their rewards ranged from naming rivers, streams, and rock formations after the high-performing team members to promoting certain individuals into leadership positions. And they spent an unusual amount of time (particularly for that era) working with, evaluating, and getting to know the Corps of Discovery members.[25]

Once such individual was George Drouillard, a French-Canadian civilian in the Corps. Drouillard quickly established himself as one of the premier hunters among the men. In the winter of 1804, Drouillard's excellent hunting skills were evident, as he brought in more meat than any other man. Clark remarked in his journal, "I scarcely know how we would subsist were it not for the exertions of this excellent hunter." Shortly after the winter, the captains assigned Drouillard as the leader of almost every hunting trip; they allowed Drouillard to develop into a pivotal member of the expedition. After thoroughly evaluating the man, the captains felt free to allow

Drouillard to develop in autonomous leadership roles. In 1805, Drouillard was named to lead an exploratory band of men into Indian territory, placing him in charge of establishing friendly relations with the tribe. For the rest of the journey, he would continue to serve as the group's lead hunter; he also translated using Indian sign language and led exploratory outings into the unknown wilderness.

Another telling example was Clark's ability to turn around the performance of Private John Collins. During the winter of 1804, Collins was caught drunk and asleep on sentry duty. The captains acted quickly and ordered fifty lashes on the bare back; only a month later, Collins would receive one hundred lashes for again being drunk and asleep on sentry duty. Still, Clark saw potential in the private. Clark acted to incorporate Collins into the workings of the organization, not push him out, as he named him head cook for the Corps. Cook was a popular position because one did not have to pitch the tents or collect firewood. Trying to further incorporate Collins, Clark placed him on a voting jury for a former private on trial for insubordination. Perhaps Clark was trying to make Collins notice his own shortcomings by placing him as jury member in another's trial. Whatever was on Clark's mind, it worked; Collins's behavior improved. By September 1805, he earned a position on Clark's hunting team, being one of only six men chosen out of the whole expedition. Instead of alienating the man, Clark instead molded Collins into an effective member and incorporated him into the successful workings of the organization.

Through the combination of directive leadership skills, constantly evaluating their staff, and facilitative leadership skills, rewarding and developing superior performers, Lewis and Clark were able to sustain the performance momentum of their agenda during even the most difficult times of their journey.

Cultural Momentum

One of Lewis and Clark's true leadership gifts was their ability to employ a range of approaches to reinforce the purpose and direction of their agenda. The two-year expedition had some very clear changes in their operating environment and Lewis and Clark responded to those changes by maintaining a culture that could deliver on their agenda.

At the outset, Lewis and Clark were directive and clear about their purpose: to find an all-water route to the Pacific Ocean. And, at the outset, they monitored that purpose and direction with a very strict and directed approach. As mentioned earlier, they severely disciplined people who put the expedition at risk and/or the lives of their team members at risk. Like many military leaders, they strongly believed that the key to sustaining cultural momentum was to keep the mission front and center.

Once the Corps got through the first six months of the expedition and experienced working together in pursuit of their agenda, Lewis and Clark evolved their approach, and the organization's culture, into a more participatory one. Many decisions were made as a group or at least with input from members of the group. Lewis and Clark started the expedition with a group of skilled individuals and instilled them with the sense of mission and purpose. Once that sensibility was ingrained, Lewis and Clark shifted their emphasis from individual and task performance to collaborative, participatory group performance.

When the expedition reached the middle of the Rocky Mountains, the group had to spend weeks traveling through treacherous falls. The combination of adverse weather conditions, sparse food supply, and grueling physical efforts placed a tremendous pressure on the organization. It was during this phase of the expedition that Lewis and Clark found they needed to model the behavior that they expected from their organization. They went days without stopping, they went out and hunted, and they undertook small, dangerous expeditions—all with the goal of moving their organization, and their agenda, toward their goal. The group stayed focused and together through this intense, challenging period. When the Corps made it through the Rockies, they were a cohesive, mutually supportive group.

Through the highly volatile expedition, the Corps of Discovery evolved from a loose confederation of individuals to a very tight-knit group of people who shared a clear sense of purpose and commitment. Lewis and Clark's ability to adapt their approach and reinforce their commitment to the purpose of the organization was highly successful in maintaining cultural momentum throughout the expedition.

Political Momentum

A major challenge for Lewis and Clark was to sustain political momentum. To ensure the success of the mission, they constantly had to balance anticipation and incorporation. They had to know when to anticipate resistance, and know who to incorporate. They had to find a balance between their directive tendency to inhibit and eliminate opposition and their facilitative propensity to overcome opposition through incorporation.

On October 13, 1804, Lewis and Clark were informed by one of their sergeants that Private John Newman had "uttered repeated expressions of a highly criminal and mutinous nature."[26] In this instance, the commanders wasted no time in making a harsh example of the man; Newman was ordered to receive seventy-five lashes on the bare back and to be permanently discarded from the Corps. This sentence was perhaps the harshest of the entire expedition, as not only was the man lashed seventy-five times, but he also was discarded somewhere in the present-day state of South Dakota. Anticipating opposition in the future, the captains acted in a way that would make others think twice about questioning authority and about putting the achievement of their agenda at risk.

Lewis and Clark were also very strategic in their deployment of people. Throughout the expedition, the two leaders frequently split up—taking separate routes or conducting separate explorations. In most cases, with each exploration, the leaders divided up the men differently and there were always different numbers of people who took part in each venture. By managing and deploying their people in this highly variable way, it was likely to be very difficult for any group of critical mass to build up resistance or a countercoalition. As directive leaders, they understood how to anticipate opposition.

In dealing with political momentum, Lewis and Clark exercised their facilitative capacity by deflecting conflict and political resistance through very democratic processes. One clear example was in their navigation along the Missouri River. About a year into the expedition, the Corps reached a fork in the Missouri River. The north fork had the same muddy consistency that much of the previous section of the Missouri had. The south fork ran smooth and clear. There was disagreement as to which way to proceed. If they took the wrong route, it could result in several lost months in pursuit of their agenda.

Lewis and Clark polled all the members of the Corps, an unthinkable approach in a paramilitary organization. Most of the members felt the north fork was the way to go. Both Lewis and Clark, though, felt the southern fork was the true continuation of the Missouri River. Rather than making a unilateral decision against the majority opinion, Lewis told the Corps that he and a small team would head down the southern fork on an advance mission and return with a report.

Lewis and his team found that the southern fork was, indeed, the continuation of the Missouri. They came back to the base camp with enough information that enabled the entire Corps to support Lewis's decision to take the southern fork. Lewis and Clark proved to be correct and they continued on with their expedition without a major delay.[27]

Through these and other situations, Lewis and Clark proved to be uniquely capable of monitoring conflict within their organization, choosing strategies that deflected the conflict and sustained support for their agenda, and maintaining the political momentum they had built from the outset.

In sustaining momentum, Lewis and Clark used both directive and facilitative leadership. Proactive leaders, such as Lewis and Clark, understand that directive and facilitative leadership are necessary leadership tools. In sustaining momentum and keeping people with them until the end of their journey, Lewis and Clark knew which tool to use when.

Chapter 4

Structural Momentum:
Maintain Resources and Capacity

R & D was a lot easier a few years ago when venture capital was plentiful, government grants were available, our stock price was 80 percent higher, and you didn't need a prototype to get your project sponsored. You didn't even need an idea, just an idea for an idea. Everyone did their own thing, but we could come together and make it happen. A lot of autonomy, no hierarchy, and things worked out. Today, forget it. You're held accountable for every dime. You have to tell them what you're doing and it seems that you're constantly checking in with the powers that be. Sure, we get results, but it's different. I guess when you're concerned with new products and you have plenty of resources you do one thing, and when you're concerned about costs, you do another thing.

While structural momentum is central to the success of your project, it involves such obvious issues that it is often overlooked. Maintaining structural momentum means asking yourself basic questions: How do you want people to carry out the project? How do you want them to carry out the jobs necessary to execute your objective? How do you want to design your organization? Who should report to whom? How many resources do you want to commit? Who is going to control what gets done with the resources? These are the questions that lie at the heart of your capacity to sustain structural momentum. These are the bread-and-butter questions that test all managers. The problem is that there is never a perfect answer, but several possible solutions, and they are not mutually exclusive. What was appropriate to sustain structural momentum yesterday may be a disaster tomorrow. The challenge is to know how to keep your balance.

Create Hierarchies but Don't Forget Teams

Sometimes projects just fall apart and momentum dies out because no one is quite sure who is in charge. Sometimes projects fail because one person is in charge and never has the time to make decisions. Sometimes the problem is that everyone's in charge and every decision becomes a turf battle.

The issue of who had decision-making authority arose during and after Hurricane Katrina. Contrary to press reports, in the hours and days after the storm, no one in particular was lacking motivation or interest in helping those affected by the disaster. What was not lacking was a sense of purpose or the intention of getting something done. What was lacking was a sense of organization. It was obvious that no one knew who was in charge. There was a multilevel game of tug-of-war that no one was able to win. City government thought it was in charge. The state government thought it had responsibility. FEMA tried to assert its federal authority. The Red Cross had its say. There were too many chefs in the kitchen. At times it seemed that the only person with real authority was the president, but there was no way to get him to act quickly, so the whole effort fizzled out. If you want to sustain momentum, you have to make up your mind where the buck stops, and who is responsible to whom. Without some specificity in terms of who's in charge, and making it clear to everyone who's in charge, nothing gets done.

Have you heard a variation of this story? At a hospital, everyone wants to help people, but who is supposed to give the patient the painkiller? A worried family member runs up and down the hall to look for the nurse; the nurse says she has to check with the doctor on call; the doctor on call is no longer on call; and finally she finds the doctor on call, who has to check with the patient's physician. Meanwhile, the patient is in excruciating pain, and nothing gets done. Sometimes it is critical, for the sake of getting something done, to make sure that someone is in charge.

Perhaps you've heard of a nurse, seeing the patient suffering, who decides to administer a painkiller, only to be reprimanded by the doctor on call?

In another hospital example, everyone wants to help, but the obstacle is that no one is quite sure who should be treating the patient. The patient has sustained numerous injuries. The diagnostics are not clear. The neurologists claim that the patient doesn't belong to them. The orthopedic unit feels that the abdominal surgery team should treat the patient. The abdominal surgery team thinks that the orthopedic unit should do the operation. In the end, the patient dies. This is an extreme example, but with an embedded kernel of truth.

If you don't focus on who's in charge and who's accountable, nothing will get done. To minimize blatant turf battles, to avoid your initiative getting trapped by no one knowing who is responsible and who should take charge, you're going to have to deal with the issue of organizational structure: who has the authority to make decisions, who reports to whom, what activities should occur in what departments. Structure in an organization provides you with at least a façade of order. When trying to move an initiative, you need to know where in the organization you need to address your attention. Without minimal effort to create structure, you'll never be able to sustain momentum. Recall the late, great comedian Freddie Prinze who had a memorable line: "It's not my job." If it's not your job, whose job is it? If the buck doesn't stop at your desk, where does it stop? Without this specification, inertia is likely to set in, as everyone says, "It's not my responsibility; why should I take a chance?" This is the challenge of organizational design: to design a system that will allow people to know who's in charge, how to mobilize resources quickly, and know who to turn to when they get stuck. What are your choices in structuring your effort to sustain momentum?

Over the last twenty years, there has been a lot of talk about organizational group structure. Under the rubric of organizational design there's been discussion of functional organizations, web organizations, loose and tight organizations, centralized and decentralized organizations. When you cut through the chatter, one thing becomes apparent: Your choice lies someplace between hierarchies and teams. Do you want to keep momentum going by placing emphasis on a hierarchical authority structure? Or do you want to keep momentum going by having everyone work together and giving numerous groups the capacity to influence what's happening?

It's all a question of tactical choices. If you think it's important to be directive, you put emphasis on hierarchies. If you think it's important to be facilitative, you put emphasis on teams.[28] When you think of a hierarchical organizational structure, you think of an organizational chart in the shape of a pyramid, with authority flowing from the top down. It is clear who is in charge, who makes decisions, and what's what. You put a hierarchical structure in place when you have a need for tighter control and direction. Hierarchical structure is the embodiment of a directive management style.

When you create a hierarchical structure, you're sustaining momentum by placing an emphasis on predictability, consistency, and accountability. The strength of a hierarchical structure is that it maximizes control. That might mean limiting the number of people who have decision-making responsibility or reducing the number of work units. Hierarchical structure works well when you need to simply execute.

Consider President Bush's Homeland Security initiative. In response to the September 11, 2001, attacks, and with the hope of sustaining momentum, President Bush created the

Department of Homeland Security to try to tighten the structure of the country's antiterrorism activities. Up until September 11, antiterrorist activities were differentiated across a range of units, including the CIA and the FBI. It was loosely implied that efforts would be coordinated across units. September 11 exposed how the flexibility of this structure came at a deadly price of poor information exchange, limited collaboration, and erratic follow-through.

In creating the Department of Homeland Security, President Bush put in place a more hierarchical organization in order to sustain antiterrorist momentum. Bush intended that this new hierarchical structure would centralize decision-making, allow for better coordination of antiterrorist activities, and provide greater clarity for the antiterrorist work that needed to be done. After September 11, it was clear that a coordinated antiterrorism strategy needed to be put in place. Washington and the country rallied around this critical idea. The challenge, as the president understood it, was how to move the idea forward and how to sustain momentum. The president felt that establishing the Department of Homeland Security was the best way to manage for momentum.

You can see the objectives of hierarchical structure. By increasing control and coordination, Bush sought to increase the country's efficiency in identifying and responding to terror threats. You can also see how the appointment of a director to the Department of Homeland Security had the effect of consolidating power and a certain amount of decision-making control from the previously distributed power structure.

Note how, in this case, the government was operating in anything but a stable environment. But the problems were relatively clear and there was a need for clarity and efficiency in the administration's ability to coordinate and respond to terror threats. It remains to be seen whether the Homeland Security initiative will be viewed as a successful response to the uncertainties of terrorism. But it serves as a useful case for demonstrating a common situation that most organizations and individuals face—the world changes but you still need to move ahead. In this case, Bush felt that the best way to sustain momentum under these conditions was through a hierarchical structure.

In trying to sustain structural momentum with a hierarchical structure, you maintain differentiation and coordination that are critical in keeping things moving. You believe that without a chain of command nothing will be coordinated and nothing will get done. With directive leadership, people know their realm of responsibility and to whom they are accountable. On your watch, when the hurricane hits, everyone knows to whom to turn, and when the patient needs help, everyone knows the final responsibility is with the physician on call. A directive leader has a strong belief that in sustaining momentum there has to be an emphasis on action over dialogue. Without authority, nothing gets done. A hierarchical structure eliminates overlapping responsibilities and snuffs out turf battles.

Hierarchies, though, are most often criticized for their rigidity. While they may be effective at improving control, efficiency, and consistency of implementation, it is very difficult to move these structures once they are in place. Those in positions of power tend to get comfortable. The hierarchically structured organization can have a difficult time responding to changing conditions that may necessitate a change in the way the work is implemented, the way decisions are made, or the way power is distributed in the organization.

You can more effectively implement a hierarchical structure during times of stability and/or clarity. When conditions don't change dramatically—and you don't expect them to change rapidly anytime soon—you can promote operational efficiency, consistency of service and/or direction, and clear accountability for results. Also, during less stable periods, if there is a high degree of clarity about what needs to be done—and even how it needs to be done—a hierarchical structure can facilitate a focused, controlled implementation effort.

While having a hierarchical structure allows you to sustain momentum by differentiating and coordinating, having a team-centered structure allows you to sustain momentum using a different strategy. A team strategy clusters similar activities together. It supposes that the group operates more effectively when hierarchy is eliminated and the division of labor is reduced with people gathered together in pursuit of a common purpose. This orientation is grounded in the concept of creating teams rather than delineating specific roles. Proponents of teams prefer to distribute power much more broadly across their group and spread decision-making widely and deeply. And they seek to have the work performed at a local level. They believe that the people closest to a particular problem are the ones best suited to make decisions to resolve the problem and sustain momentum. Having a team structure supports this philosophy.

A more facilitative leadership style will organize around the image of groups and teams, rather than a hierarchy. While the directive leader emphasizes hierarchy to sustain momentum through control, accountability, and coordination, the team-oriented facilitative leader sees the importance of clustering activity, dialogue, and collaboration. A facilitative leader is not convinced that the chain of command is the answer. What is important is to group individuals so they share ideas, work closely together, and develop their own sense of internal momentum. The facilitative leader believes the key to sustaining momentum is the power of the group, not the power of the hierarchy.

Teams, which create the capacity to be flexible, responsive, and creative, sustain momentum through clustering and autonomy. In contrast, hierarchical structures, which emphasize clarity, consistency, and efficiency, achieve momentum through differentiation and coordination.

You will often find teams in R & D organizations, sales organizations, and start-ups. Teams allow those organizations relatively wide latitude for pursuing opportunities "out there." Having teams also enables the organizations to respond flexibly and appropriately to customer complaints, requests, or emerging needs, without losing the opportunity or the motivation that gets blocked by a more elaborate decision-making and operating structure.

Team-centered structures seem to require a lot less effort and maintenance than hierarchical structures, but that isn't the case. Indeed, team structures may require a much higher level of maintenance and control than a hierarchical structure. In hierarchical structures coordination is built into the organization. In team structures, such coordination does not naturally exist. Coordination requires a separate effort and becomes the responsibility of each member of the group.

So, team structures require a high degree of communication and collaboration to sustain momentum. If you seek to implement such a structure, you will need to ensure that people in the group are self-starters when it comes to collaboration. Because knowledge and decision-making responsibility are not concentrated and not built into the structure, team structures rely heavily on sharing information among group members to generate creative responses and to effectively deliver products and services.

Team structures are best suited to sustaining momentum in a frequently changing environment and under conditions where there is a high degree of ambiguity. When market conditions change relatively often, you will want your operations to be responsive. A hierarchical structure would not function well under such conditions. Team structures are more likely to be able to respond well to changing conditions.

Similarly, in ambiguous environments, like in the new-product development area or in the case of nascent technologies, team structures will tend to be better equipped for exploring, testing, and adapting to the most appropriate way of moving forward. This kind of experimentation and operation is much more difficult in a hierarchical group.

McDonald's showed in the late 1980s and early 1990s how team structuring could drive momentum by enhancing innovation and growth. During the 1970s and much of the 1980s, McDonald's had honed nearly every aspect of its restaurant operations, down to the ridged edges of its ketchup packets. They were the model for operational efficiency and demonstrated how a hierarchical structure could produce the desired efficiency, consistency of product, and predictability that made management and its shareholders proud.

But by the late 1980s, McDonald's ran into the dark side of "being tight." They had achieved such a level of consistency that every McDonald's looked the same and offered the same fare virtually everywhere in the world. The problem was that tastes and interests weren't the same in every city and town where McDonald's operated. McDonald's executives found that there were limits to the company's ability to grow under the existing operating structure.

McDonald's responded to the diverse tastes of its customers by restructuring its franchise operations and regional restaurant management systems. They undertook an effort to change their operating structure so that regional and local McDonald's restaurants could have more flexibility in the menu they offered and in the products they introduced. So, the McRib sandwich might not be offered in locations where that type of sandwich was not likely to be a strong seller. Or a broader menu of salads might be supported in regions where healthier lifestyles were more popular. In Japan, products like the Teriyaki McBurger were introduced that would not likely find a market outside of the country or, perhaps, the region.

McDonald's move toward team structures seemed to pay off. Same-store sales grew. Publicity and word spread about them being more responsive to local tastes. McDonald's franchise operators became more satisfied and motivated. Over the long term, the responsiveness has enabled more innovations to develop and take hold. This is a classic example of how horizontal team structures can sustain momentum during times of changing market needs.

The McDonald's case also shows that horizontal team structures may not always be ideal. When markets are stable or cost containment and operational efficiencies are imperative, horizontal team structures can drain organizational resources and inhibit consistency of product and service. Horizontal team structures are inherently less efficient and less consistent than vertical hierarchical structures.

But for those who think having a horizontal team structure means having no control, think again. While it may not be consistent with the traditional notion of control—something much more akin to the prototypical vertical hierarchical organization—having horizontal team structures is actually a system of control. But what horizontal team structures "control" are responsiveness, creativity, and flexibility. Through horizontal structure, these operational characteristics can thrive.

The challenge for your managerial competence is not to select one structure versus another, but to know under what conditions one structure is more appropriate than the other. If you want to sustain momentum by keeping control and maintaining predictability, your emphasis should be directive and on using a vertical hierarchical structure. If you want to sustain momentum by driving innovation and creativity, your emphasis should be facilitative and focus on using a horizontal team structure. Keep in mind that each structure has its limitations. If you rely too much on vertical hierarchical structures, you'll find yourself trapped in bureaucratic inertia. If you rely too much on horizontal team structures you'll soon be caught up in the quagmire of turf battles. Your managerial competence will be tested by your capacity to balance the two options.

Provide Resources but Don't Be a Welfare Agency

The Line-Ed Corporation is the creation of a merger between a software start-up and a relatively small textbook publisher. The idea is to develop online courses in three fields: medicine, business, and hospitality management. The courses are developed for the Web in conjunction with degree programs offered by established universities. To succeed in this market, the challenge is threefold. First, it is necessary to have content that is substantive enough to warrant a partnership with a credentialed university. Second, it is also necessary to have a delivery mechanism enabling students to go online at anytime, while giving students intimacy and interaction. Third, the courses have to be aesthetically appealing, with attractive graphics and all the interactive bells and whistles that students expect. Line-Ed needs to be able to present a creative, intimate, and dynamic product that is also predictable, manageable, and profitable.

John Michelin, Susan Tweedy, and Mark Liu are the core of the design team. John, a self-taught cartoonist, studied graphic design at the Fashion Institute of Technology. Susan studied theater design at Northwestern and brings her flair for presentation to Line-Ed. Mark, a semester shy from graduating from MIT, is a program designer. Their challenge is to give the Web product the look and feel of reality. All three have a fascination with the tools of their trade and identify themselves as creative artists. They feel their perspective is a bit different from that of the others in the company. They feel that their success as professional designers doing the media production of the Web courses has to do with their having the newest software and latest hardware to run these applications. When the newest Apple G5 quad-processor desktop computer is released, early adopters line up in stores across the world and pay a premium price for their cutting-edge status. Software companies like Adobe Systems time the release of updates to their software to synchronize with the release of the newest computers, adding features, upgrades, and bug fixes while at the same time leveraging the increased power of CPUs. Photoshop is the industry standard for digital imaging, and Adobe knows its customers are loyal, deep-pocketed, and eagerly purchase updates when they are made available to the public.

John, Susan, and Mark are constantly pushing for the latest updates, arguing that with the newest resources, the more capacity they have to deliver the most up-to-date, high-end product. It is up to Hank Fledder, the CEO, to make decisions regarding upgrades. Line-Ed is a small organization, but Hank knows that its success has a lot to do with John, Susan, and Mark. Sustaining their momentum is critical. But Hank also understands that while the design team feels they need the best and the newest, there is also a limit to Line-Ed's resources. He wants to facilitate their activity but his directive side tells him to be cautious.

In most situations, the older gear does the job as well as the newer workstations in producing an online course, just perhaps a little slower. Hank understands he needs to balance the team's desire for new equipment with some bottom-line issues. Will Photoshop 6 do just as well as Photoshop 7 when designing a Web site interface? Will the new G5 render 3D scenes faster than the G4 desktop and at a higher quality? If a new server is installed, will the workgroup be able to communicate more efficiently and save time? If they wait to upgrade systems for six months, how will that affect production deadlines? Competent managers must always balance their facilitative desire to get their team what they need to enhance their momentum with their bottom-line directive judgment about the appropriateness of resources.

Sure, enhancing momentum requires resources. Without money, people, space, supplies, you'll go nowhere. You must be able to provide adequate resources in order to build and sustain momentum. In sustaining momentum the question you must answer is how many resources should you provide to people. On the one hand, if you want to grow and/or sustain your activities, you may lean toward your facilitative side and provide your group with unlimited resources. The reasoning here is that if the staff has enough resources, then they will be able to do what it takes to get things done.

On the other extreme, you can be directive and institute the "starvation strategy." If you limit resources so severely, people will become very creative about getting things done. In fact, if they are so resource-constrained, they will come up with better and more cost-effective solutions than they would have if they had unlimited resources. This is an attractive philosophy to most managers in organizations, but it is also a very risky proposition. What happens if people cannot find those alternative resource-lean solutions? What if the restriction is so limiting that it, indeed, puts the organization at risk?

It is great to be in a position where you can facilitate all the resource needs of your group so they can get the job done. If this is the case, you clearly are in a privileged minority. Still, there are plenty of managers who have access to a range of resources. Sometimes those resources reside within the organization. Other times, as in the case of not-for-profit organizations and of many entrepreneurial companies, those resources reside outside the organization's traditional boundaries. As you push your group's agenda forward, and try to sustain momentum, you will likely draw on these resources.

When people feel they have access to the resources they need to do their job, they are likely to have higher levels of satisfaction about their work and about the organization itself. Regardless of whether those resources actually help them do their job better or increase their performance, simply having that access can result in a continued commitment to pursuing the goals of the initiative. Most leaders understand this and are only too happy to provide their people with the resources they need.

But there may be a point of diminishing returns. The history of the American welfare system demonstrates this. By providing U.S. citizens with a safety net, the U.S. government tried to keep hardship cases motivated and equipped to get back on their feet. Over time, though, many people began to take the resources provided by the welfare system without seeking employment. The resources provided were sufficient to actually prevent the recipients from acting in the way that the government originally intended.

The same is true for organizations and resources—not that you would create a welfare system in your organization, but that you could replicate the same unintended consequences of the U.S. welfare system. If people in your organization have more than sufficient access to resources, they may be more likely to deploy those resources in ways that are not productive for your initiative. You've seen this time and again in organizations. Money is spent on seemingly unnecessary activities and materials. Ask about these expenditures and all of a sudden no one knows who is using the resources or how they were procured.

This dynamic can undermine the momentum you are trying to sustain. So, as leader, you need to consider if you are providing too many resources for a project. Momentum can be thwarted when projects are overresourced.[29] All too often, managers instinctively allocate more resources to the project, with the intention that more people, more equipment, more support will enhance the project's momentum. However, more resources mean more complexity, which requires a greater bureaucracy. While you think you are facilitating momentum, all you're doing is creating the type of inertia and encouraging procrastination that is associated with the worst nightmares of a welfare state.

By the same token, you can err in the other direction. You can starve an initiative in the name of cost consciousness or conservation. This is more likely to be the case in organizations today, with freezes on hiring and budgets. Leaders and managers overreact to undisciplined spending habits and tighten the screws to the point that projects sometimes suffocate.

You've seen this before. A new manager comes onboard and feels that the department has been extravagant in its spending and that the group is pampered, with every whim placated, and believes that what is now in order is austerity—the well-worn "lean and mean" model. This managerial behavior is predicated on the belief that holding back resources and challenging people to improvise and innovate will sustain momentum. The problem with this perspective is that holding back resources can kill momentum. So what if you decide not to upgrade John, Susan, and Mark to Photoshop 7 and ask them to stick with the G4?

When people feel that they don't have access to the resources they need to do their job, they get discouraged and frustrated. They will not be likely to sustain momentum, and certainly will not be likely to stay on your side. If you want to sustain momentum, you can ask one simple question: Does everyone have the resources they need to do the work? Vision with resource deprivation will kill momentum and drive people away.

As the leader of your initiative, you need to make sure that your group's access to organizational resources does not fall below a certain threshold, where your group shifts from being "hungry" to being "discouraged." Again, there is no science to this. There are no quantitative metrics that you can apply. It is much more of an intuitive feel and sensitivity to your group's level of motivation and creativity.

Too many managers are insensitive to this threshold. They take the idea of the lean organization and apply it to the extreme. These managers are not sensitive to the notion that there needs to be some "slack" for exploring and drawing on resources to pursue the goals of an initiative. Managers may disguise these resource constraints as "encouraging creativity." But the research suggests that placing too stringent controls over spending and access to resources raises the level of organizational stress and reduces the organization's capacity for creativity and innovation.

In giving people resources, you can't afford to facilitate every whim or restrict every paperclip. It can't be either feast or famine. You need to find that point where the limitations you place on resources do not jeopardize momentum, but enhance and inspire novel solutions, while not squandering time, technology, or support. Your managerial competence will be tested by your facilitative desire to give people the resources they want and your directive drive to limit resource waste. So, you can give John, Susan, and Mark Photoshop 7, but you promise to get back to them on the G5 once you see how well the software works. In allocating resources to sustain momentum, you can be both facilitative and directive. Facilitate what they need and scrutinize what they want.

Give Autonomy but Define Parameters

You have a plan. You know what you want to get done. You've doled out the appropriate resources. Now, how do you want them to execute? Keeping your projects moving is often about the very basic idea of how do you want them to do the job? How do you want the very activities of execution to be structured? Organizational behaviorists call this the job structure issue. If you structure the job correctly, you will be able to sustain momentum. Failure to structure the job correctly, regardless of resources, will prevent you from pushing the project forward. In trying to sustain this aspect of structural momentum, you have to balance your facilitative tendency to give people autonomy and your directive leaning to be prescriptive.

During the 1970s and 1980s, the Anzion Petroleum Company was confident that the security for the Bet-Heron fuel storage facility, with an annual capacity of 2.5 metric tons, was adequate, with armed guards at the gates, a regular jeep patrol, and double razor wire fences. Ten years ago, the geopolitical situation changed and management became concerned that the Bet-Heron site, only a few kilometers outside of a major metropolitan area, was vulnerable to a terrorist attack. A task force convened by the company recommended that a VP for security be hired to head up the implementation of a new technology-based security system. Samson Luttenberg, a retired lieutenant colonel with extensive security and military police experience, was hired to put this initiative in place.

Luttenberg had a facilitative management bias. He believed that the security "business" was so unpredictable and had so many variables that it was really up to the frontline security staff to define their work and carry out their responsibilities as they saw fit. Because of his experience in the field and a professional staff who took their jobs seriously, Luttenberg was able to lead the Bet-Heron facility effectively with this approach. Under his supervision, the new department initiated and sustained comprehensive security measures designed to prevent possible terrorist activity. Luttenberg worked closely with an in-house technology design team and security specialists to come up with the appropriate processes and apparatuses to implement the system.

At first, Luttenberg and his team were convinced that the additional, real-time data that the technology provided would greatly improve the security of the site. Luttenberg believed that as long as the security staff had the appropriate technology, they would be able to do their job better. New technologies included the installation of perimeter cameras, metal detectors, bomb sweepers, and infrared surveillance.

These improvements required that the security staff be trained to use the new equipment and security protocol. The new system still relied on the problem-solving skills and abilities of security guards. Although Luttenberg felt that technology would enhance the quality and effectiveness of his security staff's work, he worried that "too much technology" might be disruptive and create too much "routine" in work that required careful attention and constant analysis.

In Luttenberg's view, successful security was dependent on the unique capacity of field problem solvers. But it was clear very quickly that this new technology would require some uniformity and some routine to make the system effective. If there weren't some protocols and standard procedures that were followed, the security of the entire facility could dissolve into mayhem.

Some of the staff adapted well to the new technologies and were very good at using the tools available to secure the site. Others were not as comfortable with the new technology and resented the time it took to clear people through the gate and sometimes were not as careful as they should have been. Given the high degree of autonomy each security officer had in the past, each officer chose to use the technology to different degrees.

On any given day, security measures were not uniform, and occasionally, there were gaps where the facility was not as secure as it should have been, even with the new technology in place. Rather than the emergence of uniform operating procedures, what surfaced was a dangerous mix of processes— some that drew on the technology and others that didn't. Although those officers who did not use the technology were still providing an acceptable level of security at a localized level, management was using the data from the new system to make strategic decisions about security. Because they were able to bypass the system, those officers were inadvertently distorting the data that management was using. When Luttenberg realized this, he knew that he would have to put in place certain required work processes.

Luttenberg realized that he needed to become more directive in the way he managed the work processes of his team. Like it or not, they were going to have to do some things by the book, even if that contradicted the way they liked to do their work. Feeling the need to take decisive action, Luttenberg decided to radically change the role of the security staff— shifting their work from problem solving to monitoring. The security function could be readily centralized with the use of sophisticated explosive detectors and high-resolution cameras that would feed data and images to a central location where security staff would spend their time monitoring the activity in and around the plant in air-conditioned comfort, venturing out only when there was a visible problem that demanded immediate attention. This was in stark contrast to the past—when security officers evaluated security risk by walking around and being very hands-on and intuitive in their evaluation.

He also set up a critical incident protocol for every possible situation. When something needed immediate attention, the procedures were flashed on the monitors, so the staff knew immediately what next steps were to be taken by whom. While this new routine and strict procedural requirements seemed to correct the mistakes of certain officers, they opened up another can of worms for a larger group of seasoned veterans. Since their daily tasks were now changed to monitoring gauges and viewing screens, a large number of once very effective security officers became complacent, inattentive, and removed from their primary duty of security. They simply couldn't "do" security by sitting in a comfortable chair in front of data.

In trying to sustain momentum, you have to keep in mind one of the cardinal rules of keeping people on your side: People want autonomy, but they also need parameters and limits. Your facilitative inclination may tell you to give them as much autonomy as possible, while your directive inclination may tell you to specify what they do and restrict their autonomy. Managerially competent leaders, who know how to sustain momentum, do both. They know when to routinize through job descriptions and detailed specifications. They know when to give the worker autonomy and make the job as flexible as possible. In the first instance, momentum is sustained by breaking up the job into specific tasks. In the second instance, momentum is sustained by making the job into a creative, problem-solving activity.

Successful leaders keep momentum going by asking how much autonomy workers should have. Should they be encouraged to find new ways of solving problems or should they solve problems by following a set protocol? How is the balance struck between designing jobs with a task orientation and jobs with a problem orientation? It is easy to say that in a stable, nonturbulent, economically predictable universe, it is prudent to establish or create jobs with a task orientation. But what happens in this more turbulent world, when it is uncertain how things may appear around the corner?

Advocates of sustaining momentum through routinization of work processes seek a high degree of control and direction over the work that gets done in their group. Routinized work processes are, perhaps, the most common way of sustaining momentum in organizations, particularly in manufacturing and other line production organizations. Routinization of work processes attempts to maximize clarity about how work should be performed in the organization. Employees working in organizations with a simplified approach tend to be more focused on carrying out well-defined tasks.

There is a tendency for leaders to want routinized work processes. Indeed, it would be nice if all of our work could be codified and described in a fairly concise user's manual. But the reality is, as mentioned earlier, that most work today has shifted to processes that involve more problem solving. As such, if you try to sustain momentum by assigning tasks and routinizing activities in areas where you should be giving autonomy and creating problem solvers, you'll find that the work is not getting done with the quality or at the pace you'd like.

The management-consulting industry demonstrates how routinizing work processes can help improve profitability and growth. In the early 1980s, Accenture (then Andersen Consulting) had been growing its technology-consulting services rapidly. At the time, though, each project was approached somewhat differently than the next. It was then that the combined pressure for growth and for profitable projects drove Accenture's leadership to develop a standard consulting methodology.

By the mid-1980s, Accenture had developed Method One, its primary technology-consulting methodology, which provided a standard approach to analyzing an organization's information system. By applying Method One to each technology-consulting engagement, management believed it would be able to deliver consistent service, a streamlined approach to improve project management, and a consulting model that would be cost-effective and profitable to the firm.

Accenture's Method One was taught to every employee and every new hire. Even though the nature of the consulting work was far from a "routinized" work process—every client was different and every problem had its own unique aspects to it—Method One gave the firm and its consultants a language, approach, and process that enabled the firm to be consistent and cost-effective. And though Method One was criticized as being too "cookie-cutter" in its approach, the consistent methodology allowed the organization to achieve unprecedented growth profitably and with a consistent quality of service.

Task-oriented work is best suited to sustaining momentum under conditions of stability and for processes focused on efficiency and productivity. When conditions are stable, there is little need to change the way work is done. Tasks can generally proceed unobstructed and there is likely to be relatively little incentive or motivation to change the way things are done. Similarly, when efficiency and productivity needs are high, there will be much greater emphasis placed on operating with tight work processes, which will contribute to an orientation toward mass production and routine.

When trying to sustain momentum, routinized work processes will generally not do well when your group is going through periods of change or when change will require that you do things differently. It is during these times that you hear comments like, "What's worked for us in the past is no longer working." Routinization does not accommodate a fundamental change in the way work gets done, unless it is a change toward a systematic or prescribed way of doing the work. But when your group's focus is on consistency and stability and the environment introduces variability and changing needs, simplified work processes can break down.

The most progressive groups today—those that push the innovative envelope and those that provide highly adaptive services—require workers who are much more self-directed than in the past. Today, jobs are problem-solving positions, rather than task-implementation roles. They require workers to assess situations quickly and to act in a way that satisfies the customer and/or generates new possibilities for the business.

Think about flying an airplane. A friend of mine, a pilot, once told me that the way he trained was so much by the numbers that even I could do it. Sounds like a tight work process—very mechanistic. But what happens when I am flying over the Atlantic, I hit a storm, and my needs move from the task of flying the plane to one of solving the problems that a storm creates for the airplane? The same goes for groups. In which situations do you need task-oriented people versus problem solvers? Who will be your innovators and where will they reside? Where do you need maximum efficiency in your business? Move your organization's jobs toward one extreme and you are pulled to the other. Finding the right balance is difficult, but crucial for implementing your business strategy. And, much like flying an airplane, it may seem that in organizations routinized work processes are appropriate to keep things going, when quite the opposite may be true. It may be that giving people discretion and autonomy provides them with flexibility of action and the capacity to respond to different demands.

When you respond to uncertainties by giving discretion and autonomy, you are making a statement that you aren't sure exactly what's around the corner and you delegate that decision to the people doing the work themselves. This is a problem-solving orientation, rather than the task orientation of routinized work processes. The underlying premise of this approach is that given autonomy, more appropriate decisions will be made and there will be a continued sense of involvement. You will be able to sustain momentum and keep people on your side.

Giving people discretion and autonomy works best at sustaining momentum under conditions of volatility and ambiguity. When you are unsure exactly how the work is best done, you will want to empower those who do the work to actually define the work. This shouldn't be a radical concept for most leaders. Then why doesn't every manager do it? Many are uncomfortable admitting that they don't know how to handle a particular problem or cannot define a process that can be uniformly applied, and hinder momentum by not giving others discretion and autonomy. But when uncertainty is high and when uncertainty has permeated the organization, loose work processes can be a much more effective approach to getting things done than routinized processes.

Conversely, when trying to maintain momentum when there is a high degree of certainty and predictability, you should not overdo discretion and autonomy. If you have one procedure to produce your products, and no desire to change it, if your market sector is specific and unchanging, if your technology is competitively robust, if you do indeed understand what's around the corner, you may want to reconsider thinking that momentum may be sustained by facilitating discretion and autonomy. In this instance you may want to be more directive and rely on routinization.

The job of technical support at Apple Computers is a terrific example of keeping things going by giving people discretion and autonomy. If you go into an Apple Computer Store, you will find somewhere in the store "The Genius Bar." The Genius Bar is a group of Apple products experts who help troubleshoot problems that consumers have with their Apple products. If the "Geniuses" determine that the problem is a hardware problem, they will arrange for repair. If they determine it is a software problem, then it is generally up to the customer to resolve those issues, either by reinstalling the software or removing an application that is causing the problem. If the problem can be fixed on the spot, the Geniuses will help facilitate that.

A customer came into an Apple store in New York, complaining that his operating system kept crashing. He was referred to Brian, one of the resident Apple Geniuses. After the customer explained the problem, Brian asked, "How long has this been happening?"

"For the last two days. It seems to get worse at night."

"Do you do anything differently at night with your computer than you do during the day?"

"Well, at night I am working at home and often on my sofa. During the day, I am in an office working on the laptop at a desk. It also seems to happen more when I'm connected to the Internet."

"Do you connect to the Internet at home the same way you do at work?"

"Uh, no. At work I usually connect through a LAN, but sometimes a wireless connection. At home, I nearly always connect through a wireless connection."

Brian proceeded to open up the computer and take out the wireless network card. "Sometimes these cards get loose. The kind of crashing you have is usually due to a poor connection with either the wireless card or with the RAM. And since your problems seem to happen more often when you are on a wireless network, let me try that."

After that didn't solve the problem, Brian said, "Let me take it in the back and reinsert the RAM card." He returned with the computer and said, "Try it tonight. If it doesn't crash, it was probably due to a loose RAM. If it still crashes, bring it back and we may need to set up a repair request."

This is the nature of the problem-solving orientation toward work processes. The problems are not always known or knowable. The problems require definition, evaluation, and proposing a solution. This takes a very different set of skills than having problems well laid out or having processes that are fixed in approach. In this case, Brian was probing for clues that would lead him to what the problem actually was. The customer may have thought it was a computer virus or a bad software program. Brian's ability to ask good questions and to understand the products enabled him to hone in on a solution. It turned out to be the right solution.

Contrast this approach to what might happen if Apple management had pursued a routinized task approach. In a simplified environment, the customer would have brought her laptop into the store and the customer service representative would have said something like, "Please fill out a form describing your problem. You'll need to leave the computer here, along with your form. We'll have a technician look at it and we should be able to get back to you in a couple of days. If it is a software problem, we'll return the computer to you. If it is a hardware problem, we will give you an estimate of what it will cost to fix it. Thank you for coming to the Apple Store."

As a consumer, which service organization would you rather deal with when you have a problem? What are the costs of choosing one work process over another? In the case of Apple's Genius Bar, the enriched work processes gives them the opportunity to solve customer problems, build the value of the Apple brand, and create satisfied customers by matching the work processes to meet the uncertainties of customers' problems. But this is not at all efficient. As leader of a group, which work approach is better suited to the challenge at hand and to the work that needs to get done? In trying to sustain momentum, the challenge to your managerial competence is finding the right balance between relying on routinization and giving people discretion and autonomy.

In the 1990s, there was this notion of the "new economy." Start-up organizations viewed themselves as engines that created value through new products. This adventure was backed up by a seemingly endless source of venture capital. On the mere whisper of an idea, no matter how unformed, resources were made available. Most start-ups were run in an extremely facilitative manner, with an emphasis on teams rather than hierarchy; an overflow of resources to R & D; and, autonomy was the mantra of the day. In the short run, the myth of the "new economy" suppressed the reality of cost. As it is often the case, reality has a way of catching up. When the bubble burst, costs emerged as the lord of the manor. While previously the emphasis was on teams and autonomy, with a fountain of resources, now hierarchical control, fiduciary responsibility, and mundane job descriptions came back on the scene. The pendulum had swung back.

This is the dichotomy between the directive and facilitative approach to sustaining structural momentum. When your concern is with innovation and new products, there is a tendency to lean toward facilitative leadership. When the organization is cost-driven, there is a tendency to maintain momentum by directive leadership. The hard reality that managerially competent leaders understand is that what goes around, comes around. Sure, you can stimulate growth and innovation with a facilitative approach and hope that in the long run new ideas and products will make you more competitive and reduce your costs. But that may never happen. You have to balance your facilitative style with a directive style that will keep costs down in the short run. But, if you constantly adhere to a directive style, thinking that cost reduction in the short- and long-term is the most critical factor, then you will suppress innovation and creativity. In this instance, over time, you will be most successful if you supplement your directive style with a facilitative style. If you don't, you'll reduce your costs but have no new products to compete with in the changing market. So, your challenge in sustaining structural momentum and keeping people on your side is walking the tightrope between directive and facilitative leadership.

Chapter 5

Performance Momentum:
Monitor and Make Adjustments

We have a niche market—K–12 textbooks, with a special emphasis on math and science. In the old days we had a lock, with little or no competition. It was all about getting the books out. It was less of a sales business than a shipping business. Now, the competition is amazing. I've got companies from Amsterdam competing with me in upstate New York. Now it is a question of getting the right salespeople in the schools and moving the product. We've done that. This new crew is amazing. I've given them more autonomy than I care to think about. They have their own cars, we cover all expenses, and resources are absolutely not a problem. The question is: How are they doing? The new program has been in place for two months and I'm not sure if it's too early to evaluate them. If I jump in too quickly, some of them may jump ship. Then what do I evaluate them on? On how they're doing the job? On the output? It may be too early to do anything, but when and how do I find out?

You have structural momentum. You know who will do what. You've given them the resources. You know how you want them to carry things out. Now, you can walk away and let things take their course, right? Not even close to right. How often have you been in a situation where projects are launched and left to their own demise? No evaluation, no standards, no feedback, no momentum.

Sure, your initiative is based on a good idea, and it's moving ahead just fine. But you have to stay on top of it. You have to have the capacity to detect when things veer off course and step in to make corrections. Even the most well-conceived, best-planned initiatives are bound to face unanticipated challenges. Your capacity to sustain momentum and keep people on your side will be tested by your ability to monitor performance and make adjustments.

Managerially competent leaders maintain momentum for their initiative by making evaluations and, in turn, making adjustments based on those evaluations. They understand that a plan is just that—actions based on a certain set of assumptions. But when those assumptions change and when actual events prove those assumptions incorrect, the most effective leaders adapt. They don't send the ship into the iceberg because their plan called for moving along that path. They revisit where they are, where they need to go, and the new set of assumptions that present themselves (e.g., if we continue on this course, we will sink the ship).

This seems like an obvious notion. Yet, time and again you read in the news about failed efforts in the boardroom and in the legislature and a pattern emerges: circumstances changed, but leaders failed to change their plans accordingly. "The ways that worked in the past no longer worked this time." Sometimes, by the time a leader realizes his initiative is failing, or dead on arrival, it is too late to take corrective action. Or a leader may ignore the obvious shortcomings of his plan and hope that problems will self-correct or disappear. Or there may be so many problems with the initiative that the leader becomes overwhelmed and freezes—and takes no corrective action.

Sometimes projects drift when you're not comfortable with monitoring and making adjustments. Other times, you just get sidetracked. The facility in Costa Rica demands your attention. You fly out for three days and when you return, another request is made by an agency in South Dakota. If that weren't enough, you're contemplating another product line. With all these demands, your eye is off the original project. The project is facing chaos. Your mistake was taking your eye off the ball. Your mistake was not to monitor and make adjustments. The question now is, Is it too late for you to regain momentum?

Concentrating on structural momentum without paying attention to performance momentum assumes that all is well with the world, that everyone has good intentions, and that once the initiative is launched—it's full steam ahead. To say this is naïve is an understatement. Nothing is more difficult than making evaluations. Nothing is more difficult than monitoring the performance and output of others to assure that things are moving on the right path at the right pace. Difficult? Absolutely. But your capacity to monitor and adjust while moving things forward and keeping people on your side is a critical test of your managerial competence.

In sustaining momentum, you, as a managerially competent leader, have to make sure that you have the capacity to diagnose the situation, and take the remedial strategy necessary to get back on course. This is not so simple. For example, in a school, what if a principal discovers that the reading scores, once a new program has been introduced, have not lived up to expectations? Is this because the program hasn't been appropriately applied in a specific grade? Is it because particular groups or individuals have applied the material not as intended—while others followed the script? Is it because the program clashes with how things have been done in the past? It is one thing to organize your effort and to build the capacity to deliver on it. It is quite another to stay on top of the progress, to assess it, and to make any changes that are necessary.

Evaluating to sustain momentum is about asking the right questions often enough, but not overdoing it, and asking them in such a way to focus your colleagues, but not destroy their motivation. Evaluating to sustain momentum means staying on top of things but not smothering your people. It implies both directive and facilitative orientation.

One way of killing momentum is digging too deeply and making evaluations an end in its own right. There is a possibility that if you evaluate people too formally and too often, you will destroy the momentum you're trying to sustain. The very word evaluation seems to be a turnoff. Terms like *annual, biannual,* or *performance appraisal* all seem to have an Orwellian sense of accountability and control. The immediate reaction is defensive. Even when the evaluation is a broad dialogue or narrative, including 360-degree feedback, there is the strong possibility that you'll waste time, create antagonism, and even instill some paranoia, all of which will counteract whatever momentum you're trying to sustain.

The formal, annual, mandatory evaluation or the politically correct dialogue between a manager and staff has the potential of slowing down your initiative. Formal evaluations that are reduced to a simple grading system may choke momentum and encourage inertia. Micromanagement, the sense that you're looking over people's shoulders or being a back-seat driver, will most likely bring your momentum to a halt due to the fact that no one will be willing to take the initiative, fearing your performance reaction. At the other extreme, you want to make sure that you don't have a hands-off attitude, where you fall asleep in the back seat of the car, with the expectation that everyone knows where you want to go.

Another way to kill momentum is by casual, lethargic, or chaotic evaluation. You know what happens: The manager comes in and asks how the team is doing. He doesn't ask any direct questions but he leaves the impression that he doesn't know what he's going to do with the information he's able to gather. Everything is roundabout with a veneer of informality. He asks, "How is the project going?" The simple answer is, "Fine." But "fine" won't give him the information he needs to keep the project moving. Too many things, too many projects, too many activities are sustained by the casual "Everything's fine."

If you don't want to lose your people, if you want to keep them on your side and sustain the movement of your initiative, you need to give serious thought to how you are going to evaluate and make adjustments.

Be Clear about the Subjective Bottom Line

In order to take corrective action you have to monitor and evaluate performance; you have to know where your initiative stands. How well are people implementing your initiative? Are you achieving the results you want? Are you reaching out to the right constituents? Are you making appropriate progress?

An important part of every managerially competent leader's job is to provide their members with clarity around the criteria they will use to evaluate process and performance (the "what" of evaluation) and the standards to which they will hold members (the "measures" of evaluation). Too few people in leadership positions provide clarity about what is being evaluated and what measures are being used to evaluate process and results.

In sustaining momentum, it is not enough to tell someone, "I am holding you accountable for production." Or, "You are responsible for the IT needs of the initiative." Don't make comments that are too broad to be meaningful. You need to define criteria that are specific enough that people understand the different domains, or areas of their work, to which they will be held accountable and evaluated against.

You would think it would be easy to decide how you want to evaluate progress; however, nothing in organizational management is more complex. Herein is the quagmire. In sustaining momentum, one of the most essential things is to be able to make evaluations, but one of the most difficult things is to know what to evaluate. Nothing will slow down your initiative more than getting everybody up in arms because they don't know what is being evaluated, or worse, because they think you're evaluating the wrong thing. While monitoring and evaluating are critical to sustaining momentum, if not done correctly, you'll drive people away and not be able to keep them on your side. You want your evaluation to be able to sustain momentum and keep people on your side.

The Hart Insurance Company decided that it needed to create a new PR and advertising campaign. The main feature of this initiative was an improved Web site as well as development of CD-ROMs that could be mailed or distributed during sales calls. David Yanowitz, a graphic designer, was promoted to oversee a design team in the marketing department to head this initiative. In this capacity, he reported to Chuck Wu, director of marketing. David brought with him three designers and recruited two recent graduates of a prestigious art school. Their charge was to create an innovative Web site to replace the company's outdated Web presence as well as create interesting CD-ROM "giveaways" that would attract clients.

David didn't really care where people worked. His main concern was the quality of the work and that it was done in a timely manner. Most of the team preferred to work out of their homes and costs did not seem to be their driving concern. Three months into this initiative, Chuck called David in and lit in to him. "I never see people in the office. Your costs are out of sight. I'm not sure who is responsible for what. It's out of control. You have to bring your people and this project back in line with the marketing division." David was caught off guard. Suddenly, he had to ask his people to come to the office. He knew that it would not positively affect the end product, and might even hinder his team and crimp their creativity. Plus, if he had to account for every nickel, dealing with the nuts and bolts of the operation would surely slow down the initiative. He felt that Chuck missed the point and was about to evaluate the project on all the wrong criteria.

David responded, "What you told me was that you wanted new products and that you wanted them quickly. We're doing that. The entire reason we are able to be so efficient is the nature of our working arrangement. The Web site had over 1.6 million hits last month. We've produced nine CD-ROMs for each of the nine prime products. Sure, our costs are high, but that's a short-term way of looking at it. Our costs are high, but our production is amazing. In the long term, our costs are going to look insignificant. It seems to me that you're switching the criteria for judging the project. Chuck, we have to be consistent as to how we're judging our progress. If we don't keep our criteria clear, we're going to slow down this initiative, if not kill it altogether. Remember, these are creative people and they're pushing hard. We'll turn them off if we suddenly change what we're holding them accountable for."

In considering what you're going to evaluate, the most important thing is to distinguish between process and output. When concerned with processes, you're fundamentally concerned with how things get done—how people carry out their work. When concerned with output, you're concerned with the bottom-line measures that indicate success or failure. A friend of mine, a long-time head of a biotech R & D group, tells me that as long as the team comes up with products, he doesn't care how they go about doing it. He often declares, "I'm results-driven. They can play around with the processes any way they want. Processes are never written in stone. If my team gives me a high-quality, on-time product, I'll stick with them. Processes are only a means to an end. It's the end that I care about."

Think of public policy. How often are bureaucrats so obsessed by making sure everyone is carrying out an initiative by the numbers that this becomes an end in its own right? How many effective development programs has the World Bank established? How many successful urban-development programs has the federal government launched? How many Homeland Security programs have been put in place where emphasis is on how the program is executed with little or no emphasis on results?

Bottom-line indicators are measures that allow an organization to maintain a competitive advantage. These measures include productivity, quality, and innovation.

When you think of measuring productivity, you think of things like dollar cost per unit, dollar sales per employee, and equipment utilization rate. If you think of measuring productivity in a school system, you think of the scores students achieve on standardized tests. If you think of measuring productivity at a university, you can count the students who went on to good jobs or the number of faculty publications. When you put in an initiative and want to make sure things are moving in the right direction, you will often measure against the notion of productivity.

How often have you heard, "We are moving in the right direction, but are we being productive enough?" There are problems with evaluating your project's momentum based solely on productivity. There are no standard ways to measure productivity. In many instances, productivity is more of a metaphor than a reality. Because of the lack of standards and norms that measure productivity rates, it is sometimes difficult to assess momentum on this basis. What does it mean to say a particular project is effective or productive? In the case of the Anzion Petroleum Company, does it mean there are fewer terrorist incidents or security breaches? Or does it mean that more cameras are watching the perimeter? How do you evaluate progress when progress is measured in terms of nonevents? Consider a high school's truancy reduction program. Should the number of truancy interventions conducted by school staff be a measure of productivity? Or would the overall dropout rate be a better indicator of productivity?

There are many situations where the indicator of productivity is difficult to apply. For instance, how would you measure productivity at a hospital? How would you identify the unit of output? The selection of the unit of output is often not so straightforward. Thus, in R & D labs, for example, the dilemma is to measure output in terms of number of publications (likely to be the scientists' choice) versus the number of new products developed (likely to be the management's choice).

Quality is the second factor used to evaluate the bottom line. Second to productivity, quality is a widely used indicator of movement in the right direction. While it is possible to objectively test products and services for quality, the bottom line is still that quality is entrenched in value. What I might perceive as a high-quality hamburger, you might perceive as inedible.

As in the case of productivity, there are many measures of quality, including product defects, customer complaints, rejects, refunds, repairs within warranty period, or service and repair cost per line. Yet simply counting the number of product defects, complaints, returns, and repairs may not be sufficient. The extent of the defective merchandise or poor service may also be critical. Thus, the severity of the complaint may mean more than the total number of complaints received. For example, a pharmaceutical company need not be flooded with hundreds of "complaints" that a new drug may cause birth defects; only a few "complaints" would be sufficient to result in the drug being pulled from the market. A manufacturer of bed sheets is not likely to respond so quickly if two or three customers complain that the dye on the sheets runs when washed.

Just as in the case of productivity measures, there is a certain subjectivity when evaluating on the basis of quality. Productivity and quality can be affected by so many factors, even those outside of the immediate control of the worker, the manager, and the organization, that to identify the precise cause of changes in productivity and quality is often a game of glorified guesswork.[30] The fact is that you can evaluate how your initiative is moving on the basis of bottom-line measures such as productivity and quality, but that doesn't mean that your initiative had anything to do with the bottom-line measures.

An alternative or supplement to evaluating bottom-line measures of momentum, such as productivity and quality, is to examine the processes that are being implemented. Sometimes the most obvious thing to evaluate is how well individuals carry out their activities—how innovative, creative, and expeditious they are. This is not just to look at productivity and quality, but also at the underlying processes that may impact such bottom-line measures of productivity and quality. How well do they implement an initiative? How well do they do the job? How creative are they? Are they striving for results? This is based on the notion that it is a mistake to become too obsessed with evaluating outputs. What you need to take a look at is process. Process is the thing you can most readily change.

Ten years ago, a New York City department store unveiled an initiative to change the interaction between a salesperson and the customer. Management encouraged salespeople to spend more time with the customer. The thinking was that time spent with each customer was a long-term investment, not just a one-shot buying opportunity. The store promoted the theme, "Go for the relationship, the sale will follow." Salespeople were to view themselves as problem solvers who could deal with the unique needs of every customer. Those that were innovative, creative, and used the time well were the ones who, over time, would show an increase in sales. But is it the case that because you do things well there will be measurable consequences?

Consider the situation where a school district introduces a new teacher-intensive reading program. If the momentum of the project is simply evaluated in terms of reading levels, you may have missed the point. If you only evaluate momentum on the basic output measures such as number of students taught or reading levels attained, you may miss the fact that the program was successfully implemented by every teacher, even though reading scores failed to go up. Teachers may be exceptional and spend all the time in the world with their students, but the bottom line may not be there. No matter how hard the teacher tries, no matter how hard a salesperson tries, there are circumstances and factors that mitigate a direct relationship between the quality of efforts they make and the consequences.

As one sales supervisor remarked after a new sales incentive program was put in place, "These people are hustling. They are doing everything we asked them to do. They bought into the idea of group sales teams, they've pushed on all fronts, but the numbers aren't going up as quickly as we hoped. Clearly, it's not them. We have the right people. We have to adjust the program, maybe change our market emphasis."

You're caught in a bind. You have a new initiative. You want to make sure the momentum of the project is sustained and keeps going. In order to do this, you need to use evaluation to gather critical information so you can make adjustments. There are two types of information you can gather—bottom-line measures, such as productivity and quality, or process information. The problem is that all this data is, at best, subjective. It's never quite clear what the bottom line is and it's never quite clear how processes should be implemented. In the context of this ambiguity, the act of gathering more information will often create inertia, hesitation, and the inability to follow through.

Sometimes if you've mismanaged the monitoring and evaluation process by not setting clear criteria, the very people you want to keep on your side and who help you sustain momentum will become timid and reluctant, and chaos—the antithesis of momentum—will ensue.

First, if you don't specify criteria, members of your group will become timid and likely seek direction for even the most obvious or mundane questions. The result is that the group will take too much time discussing next steps, rather than taking next steps. Over time, people working without clear performance criteria will learn to become dependent on the leader and seemingly incapable of making decisions on behalf of the initiative.

A second implication of unclear criteria is that people will become more reluctant to engage in the project. Yes, they will continue to show up each day. Yes, they will continue to be "part of the team." But because what is being asked of them is so ambiguous, they will lose the drive and motivation to perform. Whereas at the beginning they may have been enthusiastic supporters of the effort, over time, they will have shifted to a focus on seeking clarity and, when they do not get that clarity, to cynicism and inaction.

A third consequence of unclear criteria is chaos: your effort can become a disorganized mess—with people marching in different directions or working at cross-purposes. Over the long term, this will result in an effort that goes nowhere and group members who are constantly at odds with one another about responsibilities and actions.

When you're gathering performance information about your initiative, don't forget you're getting that information from people. Every time your request for information is ambiguous, you create uncertainty. When people face uncertainty, it's hard for them to sustain momentum. When you ask for information, they may wonder, "Why did she ask that? Why did she want this?" They'll perpetually second-guess your intention and motivation. When you specify what information you need and on what criteria the project is being evaluated, you'll ground them in what needs to be done and motivate them toward the goal of the initiative. Managerially competent leaders use clarity to eliminate one source of discontent that may kill momentum.

In addition to being clear about performance criteria, you need to be ready to change criteria when circumstances change. There's nothing more threatening to an initiative than continuing to do the same thing when circumstances have changed. Managerially competent leaders monitor the changing needs of their agenda and change people's responsibilities accordingly. Too often, people get stuck in a routine and find it difficult to move off that routine. To sustain momentum, though, you need to move people off that routine, when necessary, and help them establish a new routine, one that reflects the criteria that are now needed for the agenda to succeed.

By setting clear criteria, you accomplish two things. First, you are putting a stake in the ground that says, "These are my expectations, and failing to meet those expectations will be considered inadequate performance." Second, clear criteria help each member of the initiative decide what is acceptable and what is not in a way that is less likely to result in a highly variable range of performance. When team members object to a particular course of action or decision, they will more likely do so in reference to previously defined criteria. By setting clear criteria you are able to have more productive reviews and performance management discussions. When you, as a managerially competent leader, set clear criteria, you increase the likelihood that your project team will remain engaged with your initiative. With clear criteria, your team will be able to move things forward and get things done.

You will also need to be prepared to adjust criteria, as new information and events arise. Specific criteria exist for a certain point in time under a specific set of operating assumptions. When times change and those assumptions are no longer appropriate, you may need to revise the criteria under which the project will be evaluated. Most people believe that "high quality" is an enduring criterion. But the definition of high quality will change over time. Managerially competent leaders understand that criteria need to evolve, as the initiative evolves. And you should not be afraid to modify your standards, as needed.

Here is your bind: You have to be clear about the subjective bottom line. You want to make clear the criteria by which you'll evaluate how much progress has been made. You want to use specific and clear criteria to evaluate the bottom line. But you must acknowledge that criteria are subjective. There are many measures of output and processes, and any measure of progress is, at best, a moving target. What you consider to be appropriate criteria, someone else may view as inappropriate. Today's criteria may not be appropriate tomorrow. Evaluation is a process with many subjective elements. As a managerially competent leader, you must be well aware that subjective or not, stable or not, you have an obligation to be clear how projects and people will be evaluated. If you fail to do this, you will not be able to sustain momentum and keep people on your side.

Make Adjustments but Don't Overreact

Monitoring and evaluating are only the first information-gathering steps. The next step is to make adjustments and corrections based on the data you've collected. Now your challenge is to make the adjustments and follow through.[31]

It seems obvious—if you have data that indicate an initiative is failing, you should be able to make adjustments. Yet sometimes inertia sets in after an evaluation has been made. You put the initiative in place, and it's moving; sure, it needs adjusting and tweaking, but is it worth the effort? You already have some embedded transaction costs. You are already comfortable with the process. You wonder how much risk you're willing to take, how much adjustment you're willing to make.

George Irwin, assistant administrator at the Broome County Sisterhood Hospital in upstate New York, had put in place a network of satellite clinics to provide preventive frontline medical care to area residents. In getting the project off the ground, he had mobilized support for his initiative and immediately established structural momentum by giving units the resources they needed and staff autonomy and control over their own decision-making. Drawing on his facilitative management style, George clearly was a managerially competent leader, capable of keeping things going. Everyone, it seemed, was on George's side. After ten months George faced the reality that the time had come to evaluate where things stood. When the data came in, things started to look a little foggy.

The bottom-line figures showed that the utilization rate was below what he had projected. The doctor-patient ratios were too high. Most disappointing, the new satellite clinics were implementing George's idea in a heavily bureaucratic fashion. People were not innovative and creative in servicing patients. Things were okay, but they weren't quite there. George was caught in a bind. How could he make corrections without throwing the project off-kilter? How would he make critiques and adjustments without stifling the initiative?

He considered that if he did nothing, the satellite clinics could become money-losing bureaucratic imitations of the central hospital. But, maybe not. Maybe the best thing to do would be to leave well enough alone and see how things would shake out; it might work out in the end. But, he also thought that another option was that he could call a meeting and lay it on the line and let the doctors and staff know that what they had been doing up to this point was unacceptable. George had to be careful. He knew that overreacting could bring momentum to a screeching halt.

In nearly every organization, you see leaders who overreact. They are the ones who take every piece of information, every strand of data, and take action based on that information. These leaders seem to be unable to prioritize or filter the fundamentally important information they receive from the anecdotal, anomalous information that is pervasive in organizations. You've seen or heard it before. Someone will come into the office and declare, "We've been getting a lot of complaints (read: two) about our new software upgrade."

The overreactive leader may take that information, call up the lead programmer on the project, and demand that a new version be created immediately.

Overreacting is a strategy that leaders choose to assure that they won't be perceived as "falling asleep at the wheel." They may believe that any action is progress and that even if they make a wrong move, they can quickly correct it by remaining active. They will denounce critics with comments like, "Well, at least I did something!" Or, "The competitive environment is changing quickly. If we don't do something, we're going to fall behind."

What overreactive leaders fail to realize is that with each shift, they are sapping the momentum they've built from past action. Think of it like rolling a ball bearing down an incline. If you let the ball bearing roll untouched, momentum builds. But what happens if after the first couple of seconds, you redirect the ball bearing with your finger? Then what happens when you redirect it another second later? Then another? The ball may come to a virtual stop or, worse, it will keep moving but in a jerky motion, never really building up any critical mass. This is a metaphor for how team members experience initiatives run by overreactive managers.

People who work on projects led by overreactive leaders are likely to burn out or become frustrated by the frenetic action and stunted progress of the initiative. Too much time is spent asking—and answering—the question, "Where are we going next?" In this situation, it is difficult for the leader to make sure the work gets done and that things keep moving.

Over time, people are more likely not to do some tasks, fully expecting that priorities and objectives will change shortly. When behavior reaches this point, an initiative has lost, and is unlikely to regain, momentum. You can run around frantically saying the sky is falling once in a while, but if you do it every other day, you'll kill momentum.

When trying to make adjustments, you must avoid casting blame and attributing causality. Your goal is to make adjustments while keeping people on your side. George looked at the performance data and clearly understood what had to be done. He also understood that in making adjustments, he could not overreact. He faced one of the major "micro" challenges every managerially competent leader needs to confront at one time or another. The challenge is how to communicate the need for adjustment in a constructive way. George knew he had to get the performance information to those who could make the needed adjustments. His challenge was to give constructive feedback to assure that appropriate adjustments and corrections were made without curtailing the momentum that the satellite clinics had built up.

Making adjustments is dependent not simply on the information you gather, but also on the nuances and subtleties you project in giving feedback to others regarding the need for adjustments. It's very simple to assume that you've communicated clearly. More often than not, this assumption is far from the truth. What may be crystal clear to you may be muddled to someone else. Comments you view as constructive, others may perceive as hostile. What you may view as an essential truth, others may see as an obfuscation of reality. Your capacity to communicate clearly is essential when you make corrections to sustain momentum.

George realized adjustments had to be made. It was clear that not all the satellite clinics operated in the way they should. It was evident that some of the doctors would have to change how they dealt with patients. It was clear the administrators would have to stay on top of the doctor-patient ratio. It was less clear whether one or two of the satellite clinics would have to close. From the data he saw, there was a slight possibility that this initiative would fall apart all together. Some things had to change. Some adjustments were critical. George was going to have to give feedback without turning them off.

With the initiative in place for only ten months, George was smart enough to realize that inertia was setting in. Even the smallest recommendations would face resistance. People were comfortable with how the satellite offices operated. They enjoyed not having to operate in a centralized system. The doctors were especially comfortable being removed from the larger hospital system. George knew that he would have to be very careful how he communicated the need to make adjustments. George's first decision had to do with the channels of communication. Should he use formal or informal communication to provide feedback?

Formal, or explicit, communication means using the organizational structure to communicate. The most obvious instance of this is downward communication. George could call for a meeting of the staff of all the satellite clinics, lay out what had been going wrong with the initiative, and specify the adjustments he'd like to make. Or George could send out a number of formal statements down the hierarchy, making clear what he felt needed to be done. The problem with such formal top-down communication as a way of giving feedback is that it may achieve the opposite of what was intended. The initiative George was trying to sustain might be curtailed. While this directive style may be appealing, it may slow momentum and diminish the support for George's effort.

Informal, or tacit, communication means going outside the organizational hierarchy to give feedback. Think of discussions in the cafeteria or over the water cooler. This is termed "managing by wandering around."[32] George could hang out in the key facilities, have some discussions with the doctors and find out from them what's going on and slip in some of his concerns and ideas for making adjustments. The problem here was that this could take a lot of time and people might not even pick up on the cues. George knew what needed to be done, and for him, time was of the essence. Solely relying on this facilitative style of "managing by wandering around" was not the way of making adjustments quickly enough.

George understood that to make the necessary adjustments to sustain momentum, he was going to have to use both directive, formal communication and facilitative, informal communication to give feedback. His strategy was straightforward. He would call for a formal meeting to share his concerns and intentions and tell them about the adjustments he'd like to see made. The formal meeting would be followed up by a visit to each facility, to meet with people informally, reassure them that he still needed and wanted them in his corner, and guarantee that he would stand strongly behind the idea of satellite clinics. George understood what many leaders don't: In sustaining momentum a managerially competent leader relies on many modes of communication to give feedback.

People don't remain engaged with an initiative unless they are continually learning, being challenged, and/or have a sense that they are developing as professionals. If you want to make adjustments that sustain momentum and keep people on your side, you need to think of yourself as the "chief development officer." It is your responsibility to provide the kind of feedback that enables your group members to stay on track. It is always easier to point out the problems than to accentuate the positives. You need to be able to provide effective feedback, without having others think of you as a chronic critic. Being a "tough grader" can motivate your group members to higher performance. It can keep people coming back for more and keep them engaged with the work of the coalition and with their specific tasks. But if you go too far, and are unreasonably critical or overly harsh in the lessons you dole out, your feedback can do more damage than development. Not only can you lose their support for your effort, but that negative experience can carry over to future endeavors of those group members.

Keeping them on your side over the long term is a process of "developing others," not "devaluing contribution." When you make adjustments, keep in mind that you want to continue having people on your side *after* the adjustments are made. You want them to help you sustain momentum. Even when you are giving feedback, it is critical that you give them a sense of partnership rather than devalue their contribution.

When making adjustments it is critical that you be empathetic. This means that you view the adjustment from the perspective of others and that you understand their interests, their orientation, their fears, and their anxiety. What is most important is that you view yourself from the perspective of others. Being empathetic is not a glib "I feel your pain" attitude, but entails sitting down and delving into the feelings and perspectives of others, the specifics of the situation, and the objectives of your agenda. When people feel that you don't understand where they're coming from or that you are not in touch with their situation, they'll "check out."

You have seen this before. One or two group members may have their own quirky commitment to a particular process or item, and you're not aware of it. You come in and make a slight suggestion for change, and they feel that you're throwing the baby out with the bathwater. You didn't mean to, but you killed momentum because you didn't work out what your adjustments meant for others. You weren't empathetic.

Empathy is the best way of keeping people on your side when making adjustments. It doesn't need to take a tremendous amount of time or emotional effort to be empathetic. For most people, the right amount of empathy is simply listening. It is amazing how our multitasking, attention-deficit culture has turned the act of listening into a cherished, rare event! But the reality is that listening is hard work and a little effort can go a long way with your group members.

Implicit in the notion of feedback is the belief that giving people feedback is only for the sake of making corrections and adjustments. If you want to sustain momentum, you have to put this in the context of a mentoring relationship. Done well, the mentor provides relevant developmental opportunities for the protégé to participate in, while providing honest and constructive feedback that helps the protégé develop the skills to become a mentor of others and a leader in her own group or organization. When you give feedback as a mentor, rather than simply as a supervisor, you move a long way toward using feedback as a developmental rather than a performance evaluation technique. Such a facilitative mentoring relationship takes time, and if you don't put parameters on it, it can become an unproductive series of meetings. Having such a relationship for the purposes of feedback may be facilitative, but it does not necessarily allow for rapid adjustments.

Empathy, listening, constructive feedback are all well and good, but at a certain point, you may have to simply declare that the time has come to move on. You'll have to play the role of the evaluative supervisor who can say, "I spent as much time as I could with feedback, but now we're just going to have to make the appropriate changes and move forward. The time for conversation is over."

In making corrections and adjustments, you may not want to begin with such a directive approach. But after a time, your facilitative feedback style is going to have to be supplemented with a directive style. You want to be concerned with what adjustments can be made immediately while retaining the more facilitative ambition of continuous positive dialogue.

George was going ahead in monitoring performance and making adjustments, but he was determined to walk the tightrope between being a micromanager and a blasé, laissez-faire sort of guy. He knew he didn't want to be overly directive, using the evaluation process as an excuse to micromanage. He didn't want to look over people's shoulders and tell them every inch along the way how to think and what to do. He didn't want to be too facilitative, either, and leave people to their own devices without evaluation.

Facilitative managers assume that evaluation will kill motivation, while directive managers feel that evaluations are the only thing standing between them and disaster. Too many managers view the evaluation process as a way of monitoring—a control and accountability ritual. You, as a managerially competent leader, monitor performance and make evaluations not simply as an exercise in control, but to make appropriate adjustments and corrections that will sustain the momentum of your initiative.

Chapter 6

Cultural Momentum: Motivate to Sustain Focus

If I go to one more award ceremony, I'll go crazy. I know he's a good guy. The problem is he was an Eagle Scout. I was an Eagle Scout, too, but this guy is trying to run this like a summer camp. He has a merit-badge mentality for everything—every time you turn around there is another recognition dinner. Every time it doesn't rain we get together for a picnic. We're constantly meeting. Did you see that last week we gave out four awards for the best employee of the month? What's next? A camp song? Have a candle-lighting ceremony on the lake? I'm all for culture, but there have to be some boundaries.

So, you've established structural momentum and performance momentum. Your initiative is humming along with the appropriate resources, you're able to monitor everyone's performance and give appropriate feedback, and you're keeping your eye on the ball. Now you have to ask yourself what else you need. To sustain momentum and keep people on your side, you need to do more than give them the right resources and monitor their performance. Momentum also has to be sustained by the culture of motivation.

Motivating Through Culture

Motivation has to do with how you help others answer the question, "Why should I do it?" On the surface this "Why should I do it?" mentality smacks of the cheapest form of Machiavellianism and seems to be a model of calculated opportunism. However, all social relationships are inevitably sustained by the answer to the "Why should I do it" question. Implied in this question is the notion that we have some degree of volition—some choice. You can choose to continue a relationship or leave it. You can choose to continue working on a project or drop it. You can choose to go to the beach or stay home. A managerially competent leader who is successful in motivating others can get others to stop asking, "Why should I do it?" and get them focused on what needs to be done.

When you motivate others, you instill in them the feelings, the rationalities, and the drives that can energize them toward specific goals. Leaders who can motivate people give them the sense that they're in the right place at the right time for the right reason. A successful motivating leader is able to get people to stop wondering why they are doing something and get them to focus on what needs to be done.

The academic literature on motivation suggests that motivation is cultivated on two fundamental mechanisms: extrinsic and intrinsic rewards. Motivation built on extrinsic rewards is generally thought of as the pursuit of material resources and financial rewards. It implies a rational calculation: "If I do this, the consequence is that I will receive something of value in return"; or, "If I complete this project on time, there will be a bonus in it for me." Extrinsic rewards generally consist of material resources and incentives and are described in terms of pay and benefits. When you sustain momentum using extrinsic motivation, you're implying a formal tit-for-tat exchange: You put in so much effort and you get so much in return.

Motivation based on intrinsic rewards recognizes that part of the payoff is derived from the activity itself and that there is something satisfying about the process you're engaged in. Intrinsic rewards include a sense of self-esteem, a sense of collective, a sense of prestige, and a sense of involvement. Unlike extrinsic rewards, intrinsic rewards tend to be less quantifiable. With intrinsic rewards "feelings" count more than "commodity." When you sustain momentum on the basis of intrinsic motivation, you can't reduce everything to a formal tit-for-tat exchange. You have to appeal to people's emotions and give them a sense of purpose.

You're facing a deadline. If sales don't go up soon, there will be major implications for the Midwest division. The salespeople meet in Chicago. What kind of motivational speech do you give to sustain momentum? "It's getting tougher out there. If we don't see a 24 percent increase, we're going to have to let some people go. There are salary pressures. There are marketing pressures. We have competition from online catalogues. You have to go out there and sell. Do the job right, bring in the sales, and there is a good chance you can make that 7 percent bonus. Fail to meet the quota, and that bonus just won't be there. The game is clear: If you deliver, we'll make it. If not, there'll be no choice than to cut back." This use of threats may be an extreme case of using extrinsic tactics to motivate to sustain momentum. You're appealing to the utilitarian and calculative goals of the individual and are focusing on what they have to do to get the job done. Notice that extrinsic rewards, more often than not, create the language of "I"—"I have to do something for the reward."

Consider an alternative scenario: "We're facing hard times. Sales are dropping. We have real competition from online catalogues. We're up to our neck in trouble, but we can do it. We're in this boat together. We have a new strategy. We tried to give you as many resources as we can. Hang in there with us and we'll make it. With a bit of luck, there will be a bonus for all of us. It's a hard time, but maybe one day we'll look back and see it as a bump in the road. Let's get at it." Notice the language of intrinsic motivation. Here you're sustaining momentum by appealing to the people's normative instincts. You're motivating them by appealing to their need to be challenged; their need to be part of a team; and their need to be recognized. You're not only speaking about their job, but you're speaking of the group project. You're using the language of "we," not the language of "I."

Extrinsic rewards, such as pay, are critical to get people to achieve. You have to set up the reward structure in such a way that people feel they are being paid fairly for what they do and the pay will satisfy their material needs. This is the magic base-line equilibrium that will help you to get rolling, but will it let you go the distance and sustain momentum? This formula could be a trap. It is one thing to offer a base salary that people feel comfortable with, but what happens if for each move, gesture, and addition, you have to renegotiate the pay exchange? Taking extrinsic rewards too far will destroy momentum. It is fine to use extrinsic rewards to get people to buy in to your project. It is fine to use bonuses as a form of stimulation. Research shows that an overreliance on extrinsic rewards may negatively impact your capacity to sustain momentum.[33]

Relying on extrinsic rewards may create an environment where everything is based on exchange and calculation. It may create materialistic, alienative involvement, where each move is calculated.[34] A team that operates in this capacity creates a temporary sense of solidarity: "We're with you as long as we get something for it." But this is not the only type of commitment you need to sustain momentum.

A culture of motivation based on intrinsic rewards assumes that people are committed to your project at a level that exceeds any rational calculation of "What's in it for me?" It assumes they'll go the distance for more than just a paycheck. This is the New York Yankees' dilemma: You can pay huge salaries, but is that enough to get the team to the World Series? What if the Yankees were unable to pay these salaries? What if there were a hard salary cap that George Steinbrenner could not exceed? Or if the Dodgers returned to Brooklyn, cutting deeply into the Yankees' revenue? Your challenge for maintaining motivation and keeping them on your side is to ensure that they are intrinsically motivated to go the distance.

As one CEO notes, "The most critical thing—even more critical than getting the company financially stable—was recognizing that nobody's in this just to survive. You have to make sure there's a compelling enough story that the great people will stick with you during the difficult times, that they will hang tight for the possibilities of the future."[35] She adds that key questions a leader needs to ask are, "Do you have a team in place that can pull off that amount of change? Do they understand the company's culture well enough to use it to facilitate change?"[36]

While it is well and good to build motivation using extrinsic rewards during a growth period, how do you build motivation when things get tough? How do you motivate when there is no bonus or when you're downsizing? What you need is commitment based on intrinsic rewards. Only with intrinsic rewards can you hope your project will go the distance.

A culture of motivation addresses three critical sociopsychological needs: the need to *learn* and *problem solve*; the need for *affiliation*; and the need for *reaffirmation*.

Learning is the basic psychological need for efficacy and mastery. It is the need to feel that in your activities, you are expanding your knowledge, skills, and potential. It is the feeling of personal growth. How often have people dropped jobs or projects because they felt it was a "dead end"? Dead end equals repetition: nothing new to do, nothing new to learn, no challenges, and no upward mobility.

Affiliation is the most basic sociological drive. It is the need to identify with and be part of a group. It is the need for community. More often than not individuals are drawn to projects and activities that allow them the opportunity to identify and work with others. Group-based projects and activities retain people much longer than individual activities. Having the sense you're part of a group makes it easier to sustain momentum.

Reaffirmation is the basic sociopsychological drive for social reassurance. It is the need for recognition. It is a public recognition of what you've accomplished, who you are, and where you belong. Without reaffirmation, you create taken-for-granted feelings—people feel overlooked and underappreciated. Without periodic reaffirmation, you can stir up "Why am I here?" questions. Without reaffirmation, few people will stay on your side and you'll be unlikely to sustain momentum.

Learning, affiliation, and reaffirmation are keys to creating a culture of motivation and, therefore, to sustaining momentum. The challenge to your managerial competence is to create an organizational culture that will address each of these needs. If you want to make sure your initiative is carried out in the most expeditious and appropriate manner and if you want to make sure momentum is sustained and that you keep people on your side, you must deal with the motivational issue, and in doing so, use culture as a proactive tool. Leaders who can sustain momentum understand they must manage the organizational culture just as they maintain resources and monitor performance. Managerially competent leaders understand that culture is the glue that keeps everything else in place and they know how to manage it.

The 1980s and 1990s were the decades of corporate culture. *Culture* became a hackneyed term that consultants, executives, and HR professionals bandied about to explain all the things that a CFO or a sales executive couldn't. Culture also became the thing that everyone wanted to "change" or "redefine." Leaders wrestled with questions like: "What kind of culture do we have?"; "What kind of culture do we want?"; "What kind of culture do we need to succeed?"

By the late 1990s and into the twenty-first-century culture became this intangible that virtually every leader points to after they've exhausted all rational explanations for an organization's shortcomings or successes. When you talk of culture, it is accepted that you are referring to shared meanings and values that give people a sense of collective that establishes norms or expected behavior. Stories, rites and rituals, events, myths, and ceremonies are the "stuff" of culture.[37] But, culture is not something that just emerges while you're busy doing something else and culture is not some anthropological mist that mysteriously settles in on your organizational terrain. As someone who wants to sustain momentum, you cannot be passive about culture. You must take control of it.

According to Peters and Waterman, successful management is the art of building strong cultures by shaping norms, instilling beliefs, inculcating values, and generating emotions and a sense of collective.[38] Your challenge in sustaining momentum is not simply to wait for culture to happen, but to use culture as a motivational tool, to make sure people are committed to and identify with your projects. Managerially competent leaders who sustain momentum understand that, like resources and performance evaluation, culture is necessary to a manager's repertoire.

Create a Problem-Solving Culture but Don't Process Things to Death

Certain organizations place a strong emphasis on problem solving. A problem-solving culture is one where the questions "What went wrong?" and "What went right?" are part and parcel of everyday behavior in the organization. It is a culture where it is customary to discuss work-related errors. It is a culture where people feel free to surface problems. It is a culture where suggestions and comments are valued.

Xerox is an example of a company with a strong learning culture. When Anne Mulcahy took the reins in 2000, the company was in dire straits. Talks of bankruptcy were not only rampant, but they were accurate. For a complex range of reasons, Xerox's business had eroded and, in some sectors, virtually disintegrated. Mulcahy, a long-time Xerox veteran, replaced Richard Thoman, an IBM executive who was brought in a year earlier to right the ship.

Mulcahy had a strong cadre of support and spent her first several months developing her agenda and building the support needed to implement it. By the end of her first year at the helm, Mulcahy had restructured the company, laid out a vision for the future, and began to move the organization toward that vision. By the end of 2001, Xerox's business results began to show some improvement. Mulcahy's challenge was to sustain the momentum of her initiative.

One way Mulcahy sustained momentum for the turnaround was to reinforce a problem-solving culture. Employees' strong cultural pride in Xerox may have contributed to the firm's difficulties. Mulcahy found that many employees, at all levels of the organization, did not really understand their customers' needs, were not listening well to customers, and were overly engaged in the internal machinations of "Team Xerox." Mulcahy implemented a program that got executives "owning" specific customer relationships, and all employees focused on learning from their customers. This problem-solving culture has been key to Mulcahy's ability to sustain her agenda and Xerox's turnaround.

In creating a culture that encourages the asking of these questions, you have a choice between a reflexive or reflective problem-solving culture. A manager trying to sustain momentum in a reflexive problem-solving culture integrates new ideas in a fairly rudimentary fashion. And if the ideas don't fit in appropriately, he will disregard the ideas and continue on his way. A manager working in a reflective problem-solving culture asks how new ideas fit into ongoing agendas and initiatives. A manager who is a reflective problem solver[39] will not only evaluate new ideas on the basis of whether they are appropriate for the agenda, but will evaluate the agenda in terms of the new ideas.

Generally, in a problem-solving culture, the hope is that the actor will always reflect on the following questions:[40]

- What happened during the task—how did it go?
- Why did the things that went wrong, go wrong?
- What went well?
- What helped these successes?
- What can be done differently next time? What can be learned for the future?
- What should be done just the same, as it was such a success?

These questions can be asked in different ways, with different agendas, and with different purposes. How they are asked, and with what intent, will depend on the problem-solving culture.

A reflexive problem-solving culture will allow you to stay on track, sustain momentum, and deal with minor variations. If you have a reflexive problem-solving culture you will be able to adapt quickly to a new situation, but you will not necessarily be known for your innovation. Directive leaders will tend to be comfortable with a more reflexive problem-solving culture. They'll make adjustments, but they won't overhaul the project too quickly. They will engage in tinkering activities.[41] They are more interested in getting going or keeping moving without regard for the where and why—

they are in danger of spinning their wheels. Instead of aiming for major transformations, they will target opportunities to achieve short-term operational efficiencies. They'll focus on improving the specifics—doing what they've done before, just doing it a little bit better, a little more frequently, a little faster, or a little more cost-effectively. They redecorate, redesign, and re-engineer.

During the initial design phase of a satellite to provide Internet access for remote users, data came in from all sources: from the finance department, from marketing, IT, engineers, and likely customers. The system engineering team, in charge of integration of the project, integrated the data into their project and moved from one equilibrium to another. At each point in the project, when new information came in, they made a decision whether the information was relevant and moved on. At no point did they step back to look at their design process or at the specific design of the satellite they were designing. They were locked into a certain mindset and were only willing to make changes of a degree of variation. Theirs was a reflexive problem-solving culture. This may result in a product or process that works, but sometimes there is the haunting possibility that it will look like a Rube Goldberg contraption. Functioning, yes, but not quite as efficient as you would like it to be, nor as attractive. The satellite design team had a problem-solving culture, but they were harmed by their inability to take time to reflect on what they were doing.

A reflective problem-solving culture will allow you to make major adjustments, deal with crisis, and constantly change the processes in which you're engaged. Facilitative leaders will put an emphasis on establishing a reflective problem-solving culture, where there is re-evaluation and reflection on what should be learned and integrated each step of the way. They will be inclined toward overhauling and putting the unit on a new trajectory. Instead of eking out a percentage improvement here, or a slightly lower cost structure there, they look for fundamental transformation and, in the process, a dramatic retooling of what their unit does.

While at a fire, firefighters use set protocol and engage in reflexive problem solving. They don't second-guess the routine. However, after the incident, they employ reflective problem solving. An experienced firefighter remarks, "After a fire, we come back and hang around the kitchen. Sometimes we cook something and sometimes we don't. We get out a chalkboard and draw out what happened. Where everyone was, what went wrong. Before the next shift we may visit the site again, sometimes with the guys on other shifts, and review what went wrong and also to go over what we did right. While pretty informal, it can get to be pretty formal."

Fighter pilots also have a strong reflective problem-solving culture. After each mission, the pilots engage in many levels of debriefing. A pilot explains the debriefing process: "We're taught to ask ourselves the critical question—to understand from our perspective what we did right and wrong. Debriefing ourselves after a mission becomes a way of life. Then we get together and debrief on the next level. If we fly with someone else, we do a cockpit debriefing, a formation debriefing, a squadron debriefing. We have a whole debriefing technology, a series of steps we follow to learn what went right on a mission and what went wrong. Everybody can make a mistake, but never twice. That is what debriefing is for."

The desire to learn—and problem solve—is key to the culture of motivation, and thus, to sustaining momentum. Clearly, creating a problem-solving culture is important. Individuals will be more committed to your initiative, will help sustain momentum, and stay on your side in the context of a situation where they are learning and improving than in a situation where they are not developing. However, you don't want to create a situation where there is nonstop learning and problem solving—with people continually attending training sessions, people meeting to share what they learned, people reading every relevant journal article—and where no work is getting done. A little bit of learning is a dangerous thing, says the sage. Also, too much learning in the workplace can be just as dangerous by slowing down momentum.

Problem-solving cultures are sometimes reduced to perpetual reflection, where everyone is self-reflecting, having their say, meeting with constant discussion, and slowing things down to a snail's pace. The line between perpetual learning and procrastination may, at times, be thin. There has to be a time when you have to stop learning and problem solving and move ahead. The managerially competent leader knows that learning and problem solving are done under the restriction of time and resources.[42] There is simply not enough time to learn everything and come up with the perfect solution.

Sometimes you have to stop being reflective and start being reflexive. You have to stop thinking and start acting.

To sustain momentum, a managerially competent leader must be able to balance both reflexive and reflective learning.

Pump Up the Collective but Don't Forget the Individual

It's one thing to say that a problem-solving culture will help you sustain momentum by appealing to everyone's sense of development. A problem-solving culture predicated on open discussion, candid criticism, and honest dialogue is ultimately dependent on trust. A culture of motivation cannot be sustained without a sense of trust. From where does trust come?

When an F-16 pilot is out on maneuvers, one of the first things he does is to buckle in his harness to make sure that in case he ejects he is lifted out of the cockpit in his seat. There is no way that his act of buckling is monitored. There is no way that anyone would know whether or not he does this. He is under his own canopy. One day, a pilot forgets to buckle it— who will know? The culture is such that during the debriefing, no matter how embarrassing, he shares the incident with his colleagues. As this particular pilot said, "When you are up there no one sees or hears you, with the exception of all the guys in the squadron who are there all of the time."

A fire rages in Brooklyn. The truck arrives and everyone has an assignment and everyone is supposed to stick to his or her assigned task. Mack has the roof, but on his way there, he hears someone screaming in the backroom. Although two firefighters are directly behind him, he runs to the backroom. Even though his intentions are good, this isn't his job. Mack was supposed to be on the roof. In the meeting in the kitchen afterward, he is criticized and reminded that sometimes in a collective the individual road can lead to hell for everyone.

A surgical team is operating on the large intestine. Three doctors, one who is the chief of surgery, and two surgical nurses are present. A half-hour into the operation, unforeseen difficulties arise. While there was a plan before the operation, improvisation is now necessary. This demands on-the-spot learning. The chief of surgery asks for comments on the situation, and the first response is from the most junior doctor. At a moment like this, all learning is public and all knowledge belongs to the group—and such sharing demands trust.

In the first case, the pilot didn't have to say anything. No one would have known. In the second case, the firefighter had very good intentions, but sat still while he was being criticized. In the last case, the junior doctor was not as experienced as the others, but he trusted his colleagues enough to provide his own input. Embedded in each of these cases is the trust that emerges through an affiliation with the collective. Not only do you identify with yourself and your job but also you identify with the group. Not only are you motivated by "what's in it for you" but you are also motivated by what the group expects of you. What is important is what the individual does on behalf of the group. What's important is that when taking action, the individual understands that his self-interest is served by the group's interest, and that his job is important, but only in the context of project or collective initiative.

No company has used the collective more effectively than Disney World. The company makes all members of the organization active participants, involving them in the creative process that has led to the company's success. All company members attend a "Disney Traditions" orientation where they learn about the company's history and begin to understand the company's vision. Members of the company are not employees, but "Cast Members," and they are constantly encouraged to improve their performance by being creative. The company's strong collective culture forms a base for affiliation, which allows for criticism, development, and a generally proactive learning culture. Without the sense of collective, there can be no learning culture.

Affiliation is a key aspect of a culture of motivation because it allows the group to sustain momentum. Affiliation is best achieved while establishing a sense of community. As your agenda evolves, you will almost certainly need to assess if your group has the sense of community needed to succeed. When you establish community around your initiative or activity, you're creating a sociopsychological sense of group affiliation and associated identity. People have a sense of common identity, common purpose, and emotional ties.

You hear people who closely identify with their group say things like, "I work for Disney," or "I work at Ladder Company 52." You also hear people talk about a sense of affiliation: "We're a brotherhood." Or you hear words that indicate a common purpose: "We're in it to win." Or, "We're going to take it all the way." Lastly, there is the vocabulary of emotional ties: "I love these guys."

A strong sense of community will enhance momentum. People who feel this sense of community will stay on your side and go the distance while waving the group's flag even beyond work hours. They will defend the group's actions and show explicit pride in its accomplishments. They will go that extra mile for the group beyond their job description or beyond what's on their performance management grid. They offer up ideas and participate in meetings that may not necessarily relate directly to their work. They try to be good "citizens." They demonstrate commitment to the group and its mission by putting the interests of the community above self-interest for specific decisions.

You've seen the positive impact of the collective. The team has a deadline, and for two weeks they all have been working into the night—not because they have to, but because they want to. They are focused on their project and gain emotional strength by hanging out with their peers and are generally excited about moving things forward as a group. The collective has become greater than any individual and a source of sustenance. When you have a strong collective, you have immense energy to push your initiative ahead. A pumped-up collective may be great when things are going well. But sometimes the collective is simply a burden. Obviously you can't include everybody all the time. Doing so would slow down your momentum and open up the potential for unnecessary criticism, too many discussions, and inertia. Sometimes the collective with its implied sense of unity and consensus is a burden.

At one point in the history of your initiative, a sense of affiliation and collective may be a great way of maintaining momentum and keeping them on your side; at another, it can be quite a different thing. If the business environment requires restructuring and/or layoffs, the impact on a collective can be devastating:

We were working out of my apartment in Chelsea. You can imagine what it was like to have the two of us design and assemble boots for urban cowboys. It was a riot, we used to walk around and look at people's feet and sketch out ideas. After a few months, Samantha joined us, then Irv. When Leon came onboard, we were on a roll. We were able to rent loft space on Houston. There were no weekends, no vacations, and few breaks. We were in this together. Even as we began to grow, we were able to keep that close sense of family as part of our work. After about three years, we had about seventy people. We could argue and push each other. It was wonderful. People put new ideas on the table all the time. They always went the extra mile. No one ever did big-money calculations. It was like the three musketeers, all for one and one for all. And then, crash time. We just couldn't sustain it. The Chinese competition, less money, fewer Wall Street bonuses, and fewer people drawn to our styles. Boots stopped being in. Personally, I think we were

killed by the return of the clog. Now what were we going to do?
It became really painful. The ship was going down and there
were only a few seats on the lifeboat. Who in the family goes
and who in the family stays? It would be easier if we weren't
such a family.

The "Internet families" that were pervasive throughout
the 1990s were terrific when coffers were overflowing, stock
prices were soaring, and when options were well above
water. But what happened after the market peaked and business models were hard to find? Leaders had to dismantle
those "families." Even large companies had to pare back and
lay off staff. And what happens when you lay off people in
an organization where employees have deep affiliation with
one another? Morale declines. Productivity suffers. The
very assumptions that drove people to join the group—and
thrive in it—are called into question. The risk you then face
is that the community that was integral to your initiative
now no longer works for the individual members. You begin
to lose your best people and find it difficult to get back that
momentum that you once had.

Another risk in using a sense of collective in sustaining
momentum is "groupthink."[43] Because the collective values
conformity, unity, and loyalty, the group will do everything
to maintain the sense of collective, which sometimes leads to
regrettable decisions. Collective groups, by definition, have
a sense of cohesion, which is why they talk of "we." That
also means that they have certain expectations regarding

criticism. That means there are serious pressures to conform, to watch what you say, and to reconsider before you make objections. If you rely too heavily on a strong sense of collective to maintain momentum, the problem is that while momentum may be sustained, it can go the wrong way.

A well-known example of groupthink is the Challenger disaster. Before the launch, one engineer at Morton-Thiokol warned that the flight would be risky. The specific concern was that launch temperatures would affect the O-ring seals. While everyone knew that the O-rings were critical, and that their failure would be catastrophic, NASA personnel, with their traditional can-do attitude and collective rationality, pushed for the launch, with tragic consequences.

In the context of a strong collective, you may feel invulnerable and certain that your initiative is the right one to pursue. That is great in terms of establishing momentum, but what if you suddenly realize your initiative is going the wrong way? How easy would it be for you to raise your hand and say, "Excuse me, guys, I think we have to take a look at this again"? In a strong collective there is pressure to muzzle disagreement. There is a sense that what is important is group consensus. If the collective is too strong it will not create a reflective learning culture, but an oppressive nonlearning culture, where courses of action are rarely re-evaluated, where alternatives are seldom considered, where factual information is dismissed, and where challenges to policy are viewed as mutinous. If you're not careful, the collective culture you put in place to sustain momentum will kill it.

The collective community implies a paradox, which is embedded in the origin of the word *community*. The Latin preposition *com* implies "bringing together" of more than one. *Unis* implies the number one. A community, therefore, implies "one of many."[44] Managerially competent leaders sustain momentum by fostering the individual identities of their community members. They understand that the individuals on their team need to maintain their individuality, a strong sense of self, and a meaningful personal identity. The most successful leaders seek a balance, which creates a strong and powerful sense of affiliation, and allows and encourages members to create and maintain their own individuality and identity.

Although it is politically correct to talk about teams and group efforts with gusto, if you take that rhetoric to the extreme, you end up denying individuals some of their basic needs at work. So, you need to make sure that you are giving individual group members some individual responsibility, which will enable each person to define their role, to tie their work to the broader agenda, and allow each individual to realize, and have some degree of control over, their successes and failures. Talk of teamwork is nice but it is by no means the only key to leading a successful group over the long term.

Remember Tommy Lasorda, manager of the Los Angeles Dodgers (1976–1996)? Lasorda is famous for saying, "My heart bleeds Dodger blue." Put in a more academic context, Tommy Lasorda's identity was intertwined with the Dodger organization. He didn't simply identify with being a major-league baseball manager. He was the manager of the L.A. Dodgers. Lasorda tried to create a community where the Dodger players also "bled Dodger blue." It was that sense of community, in part, that pundits pointed to as a key to the Dodgers' highly successful string of world championships and World Series appearances between 1974 and 1982. Lasorda was able to keep the players on his side by reinforcing their common affiliation with the organization.

Lasorda understood that free agency was flourishing in major-league baseball in the 1970s and 1980s. New players would arrive each year and some well-liked and valuable players might leave. Lasorda didn't try to create a collective in the sense that each person grew inextricably close to one another to the point that specific players might not be able to play well without each other. That would have been a disaster for the organization and for Lasorda's ability to effectively lead the group over the long term. Instead, Lasorda focused on the Dodger brand (uniform) as the unifying source of affiliation, where being part of the organization was, in effect, being a valuable part of the community and leaving the organization was unfortunate, but not crippling to the team's sense of community.

When establishing cultural momentum your best bet is to recognize the individual within the group. Think of a jazz band. There is a pretty set protocol onstage. The group gets up there and they play the melody or the "head" of any given tune. Then, in turn, each player does his or her solo—first the bass, then the saxophone, then the piano, then the drums.

Then they come back together and play the head again. There is something in this image that is a lesson in sustaining momentum. The individual gets credit but the group doesn't lose its identity. Within the parameter of the collective, there is opportunity for creative rejuvenation and breathing room.

Managing the organizational culture for momentum, you may want to pump up the collective. Talk about "we." Keep on heralding, "Together, we're moving forward." The collective will spur them on and give them strength and courage. The collective is where momentum lives in its most mystical sense: the sports team, the political party, the cutting-edge R & D group. That sense of collective demands loyalty and adherence to norms and expected behaviors. Because of the danger of taking the group too seriously, the fear of criticism, and the inertia of groupthink, the collective may be the very place where momentum dies. They won't be on your side because it all became too much about the "we." In sustaining momentum, a managerially competent leader pumps up the collective but never forgets the individual.

Celebrate but Don't Worship Idols

In maintaining cultural momentum it is critical to fulfill the need for learning, the need to affiliate, and the need for reaffirmation. Reaffirmation is the public recognition of who you are and where you belong. People need the sense of recognition; without it, they feel like they are taken for granted. Even in the most collective setting, a social being wants the sense that accomplishments are celebrated and recognized. This doesn't mean that in sustaining momentum you constantly have to slap people on the back or always give them gold stars to hang on the refrigerator. But it does mean that those little gestures, ceremonies, and rites often reinforce culture as a way of sustaining momentum.

Through rites, rituals, and ceremonies, the organization not only rejuvenates and reinforces its central ideals and beliefs, but it recognizes the contribution that employees make. Mary Kay Cosmetics is an example of an organization that uses culture to constantly reinforce high-performance expectations while recognizing and rewarding individual achievement. Corporate meetings, for example, are marked by fancy settings and gift presentations (pink Cadillacs!) to star salespeople—rituals that draw attention to organizational commitment. These ceremonies take moments to provide a sense of focus and cohesion and reinforce corporate goals for employees. However, the celebration goes beyond just the lavish pomp and drama that cements an organizational view—it gives group members a sense of purpose to reach their full potential and lets them feel a sense of individual accomplishment.

How do you make the culture of motivation happen? You need to use the tools of reaffirmation. You have to know how to use symbols to get the message out about why people count, what people have done, and how much progress is (or is not) being made. In order to sustain momentum, you must make sure that your organizational culture of motivation lives not simply in the heads of managers, workers, and customers, but in the everyday reality of gestures, rites, rituals, and ceremonies.

Tone is the emotional sense of a relationship as expressed through informal cues such as gesture and play that fill in the gaps of everyday life. Gestures as a form of nonverbal expression in the workplace are critical: winking, nodding, frowning, and smiling. Gestures are often embedded with meaning.

> *Cynthia:* It's been driving me crazy all day. She's the head of HR. She knows the team assignments are coming down. She walks past me. No eye contact. Cold, steel silence. It was even awkward for me to say good morning. I come around the bend and see her assistant. He's all smiles and full of good mornings. What am I supposed to make of it? Will I be heading the new team or not?
>
> *Tom:* Look, Cynthia. You're not supposed to make anything of it. Just ignore them.
>
> *Cynthia:* I'm looking for interpretation and you're telling me to ignore it.

Organizational life is interpretive. You're constantly trying to figure out the meaning behind statements and subtlety behind cues. If you want to use the culture of motivation to sustain momentum, beware of the little things, such as intonation and body language. An informal high-five, slap on the back, a half-smile, and eye contact all send out messages. You can kill momentum by sending the wrong message at the wrong time.

Playing is another form of making gestures. Leaders who find opportunities for play and fun at work reaffirm the sense of collective. Perhaps it is by telling jokes and drawing out people's sense of humor. But it may also come from little games or challenges that you present to people. One executive used to have a table full of knickknacks, like tops, puzzles, bendy figures, and small puppets, in her office. She found that having toys out on the table encouraged people to play with them when they came into her office. The toys had the effect of distracting her group's members from sometimes tense situations, enabling people to better manage their nervousness, and, when things were going well, giving them an opportunity to stop and play during the day. The toy table didn't lessen the seriousness of the work that needed to be accomplished or reduce the respect that group members would give to their leader. It just infused a modest sense of fun in the work environment—enough to sometimes diffuse potentially big blowouts. This isn't to suggest that you go out and buy Etch-a-Sketches and Rubik's Cubes for your office; it is meant to encourage you to think about little ways that you can infuse some degree of fun into the daily or weekly routine.

Another way of reaffirming the collective is through stories, myths, and legends. Organizations will offer such devices to inspire people, keep them focused, and to sustain momentum. Stories take different forms, such as the "I remember when story": "The last time we tried a project like this, things were a lot tougher than they were today. We had such time pressure, fewer people, and the weather was absolutely out of this world." Such stories are often associated with certain industries, like construction.[45] When older ironworkers talk to apprentices to get them motivated, they tell them:

> *You guys don't know how good you got it. Today, you have these itty-bitty impact wrenches to snap out these bolts. When I started, it took four men to put in a rivet, two men to put in a high-strength bolt, and two guys to fasten the bolt. Now you do it all with a little impact wrench. You guys got it easy.*[46]

Then there is the hero story, that worker who serves as a role model—sometimes real, sometimes mythical, and most times a combination of both. Horatio Alger is the prototype. Rockefeller is the myth. Bill Gates is the contemporary role model. When times get tough for a steamfitter, usually at three in the afternoon on a blistery February day on the twenty-first floor, with the wind blowing between the crossbeams, a gang leader will tell the story of Three-Fingers Murphy to keep the momentum going. Three-Fingers Murphy would lug cast iron radiators up the stairs before there were construction elevators. This guy got hernias every week, but nothing stopped him. Breaking his arm was part of his job description.

This was real labor. By hearing of the feats of Three-Fingers, the team is motivated to move on.

Managerially competent leaders reaffirm the individual and the collective through the use of stories. They are sharing a sense of tradition and context while conveying to each individual that they are part of something bigger than themselves. The problem with such stories, when used by an incompetent manager, is that they can become a litany of "I remember when," which elicits a "Here he goes again" response from the listener. You know the reaction; it is the same as when your parents said, "When I was your age . . . " If you're not smart in using these stories well, you will not sustain momentum; you'll destroy it as people shrug their shoulders in indifferent dismissal. Some managers tell the same stories over and over, to the point that what was intended to be a facilitative activity becomes a directive activity. Managerially competent leaders understand that in telling the story, they have to keep in mind the frequency with which they tell the story and the tone. Tell the story too often and too formally, and it can easily become an implicit directive. Tell the story selectively, keeping the tonality informal and playful, and it becomes a facilitative motivating device, helping you to sustain momentum.

Ceremonies are another way of sustaining momentum through a culture of motivation. The New York City Fire Department gives the James Gordon Bennett Medal for gallantry above and beyond the call of duty. Wal*Mart posts the photograph of the Employee of the Month. Cornell recognizes the outstanding mentoring teacher. Ford Motor Company salutes its top employees with the Henry Ford Technology Award for technical achievements and innovations. Chairman and CEO Alexander J. Trotman (1993–1998) described the award as "The company's Nobel Prize, our Pulitzer, our Academy Awards, all rolled into one."[47] Everyone knows that salesmen routinely receive recognition. Awards are a way of sustaining momentum by recognizing accomplishments and reaffirming that the group and the individual have made a critical contribution, gone beyond expected duty, and are a critical part of the initiative. Awards are a mode of positive reaffirmation.

In some hands, such public recognition, if done with the tonality of humor, is a way of goading people on. The tongue-in-cheek motivators bring focus to tasks and accomplishments without ostracizing. Among the New York firefighters, there are several such awards: the Square-Rooter Award, to acknowledge the person that divides everything for himself at the expense of others and never for the group; the Minuteman Award, to recognize the firefighter who shows up just in time and goes home just in time and does no more or less than what's expected; and the Springer Award, to the firefighter who never reaches in his pocket for anything. These awards, while given with a light touch, try to drive people back into the collective and get them back in the game without formal sanction.

Rites of passage are another important tool for sustaining momentum through a culture of motivation. People stick around when they see the benefits of membership. And what better marketing for your initiative than showing how people actually succeed as part of your initiative? When you announce promotions, celebrate retirements, welcome new members, you are recognizing how people are important to your community and you give people a sense and desire to achieve their next rite of passage in the organization. Sometimes that even means celebrating someone leaving the group for a bigger position or unique opportunity. Showing others that these opportunities exist increases the value of your group and it helps you sustain momentum and keep people on your side.

Another ritual is "getting together." More and more you hear of people getting together—the labor economists get together at the faculty club, the HR group gets together for breakfast, the CFO gets together with the division heads, the air force pilots get together on the beach for a game of volleyball. The notion of getting together, while on the surface appearing to be informal and spontaneous, is an emergent motivational tool that managers can use to keep things moving.

The tonality can be informal and almost intimate. You don't announce a get-together; you invite people to a get-together. "Will you be at the game on Friday? There are some things we need to discuss." Or, "We should really talk about the Xerox contract; will you be at the lunch at the club?" These get-togethers are informal mechanisms for keeping focus. In the hands of a clever facilitative leader, these informal get-togethers are a way of maintaining focus. Directive leaders sometimes make the mistake of transforming these get-togethers into meetings. Now, every Thursday afternoon the labor economists have lunch at the faculty club. The HR group has a breakfast meeting every Tuesday. Once every two weeks the CFO meets with all the department chairs. The pilots meet at the beach every Friday for volleyball.

When get-togethers become standing meetings, they can become oppressive rituals. You'll be asked not, "Will you be able to come?" but rather, "Why weren't you there?" The reaffirmation of collective becomes the suppression of the individual. What you hope would sustain momentum and keep people on your side becomes a source of alienation and cynicism: "I am so sick and tired of these volleyball games, but if I don't show up . . . forget it, I don't have a choice. I have to show up." A picnic that you can choose not to go to can sustain momentum. A picnic you have to go to will destroy it. Smart managerially competent leaders have a good sense of boundaries. They know when culture stops being a motivating tool and becomes an oppressive tool.

Wanting to be reaffirmed and recognized is part of who we are. As such, rites, rituals, and ceremonies are something that everyone appreciates. Public recognition is sometimes the best kind of recognition when sustaining momentum. But what happens when public recognition becomes an end in its own right—when it becomes simply another case of empty accolade? Joe had been in charge of the IT group for the last six years. He had been in the organization for fourteen years. He was a hard worker and a top-level engineer, but a little bit of a control freak. He insisted that everyone report to him and speak to no one outside of the division. Cross him at your own peril. Last year Joe was recognized by the VP for product development and given the regional award for innovative leadership. Everyone showed up at the ceremony, but many sat there with a sense of cynicism. As one member of his group said, "I understand the VP wants to give him an award, but innovative leadership? Save me. This is just his attempt to get him in his corner. At least it's a nice dinner."

If you're going to be effective in building a culture of motivation, make sure that you use the tools of reaffirmation.[48] Make sure that the rewards, ceremonies, and celebrations are not idols or empty of meaning. All too often, the tools of reaffirmation can become items to be collected with the original intent long forgotten. Gatherings, events, rituals, and rites foster celebration. Celebrations make people feel good about where they are and what they are doing. If you celebrate too much, with too many awards for every distinction, the meaning can be lost. If you don't take time out to celebrate at all, you deprive your people of an important source of energy. Find the right balance and you can sustain energy, engagement, and momentum over the long term.

A culture of motivation is critical in keeping your group focused and moving things forward. It sustains the collective and provides both extrinsic and intrinsic rewards by giving people an opportunity to grow and to learn, by encouraging affiliation with the group and providing them an opportunity to be reaffirmed and recognized. In the hands of a leader who is too directive, culture can become the blanket that covers the organization and smothers creativity. Some leaders are so obsessed with culture and so concerned with consistency with organizational traditions that the end result is worship of the culture itself. In this situation, the forces of learning, initiative, and creativity are inhibited. The very culture that is meant to sustain momentum will make them feel oppressed and overwhelmed. A facilitative leader uses the culture of motivation as a device to connect individuals with the goals of the initiative. In sustaining momentum, a managerially competent leader facilitates a sense of belonging and reaffirmation.

Chapter 7

Political Momentum:
Mobilize Support and Anticipate Opposition

> *We were doing so well. We had the resources. We had the right people. I was giving them feedback. We were playing volleyball on Fridays. There were only six months to go on this project when it just fell apart. I should have known. I should have kept my eyes open. I should have incorporated that IT guy a long time ago—or I should have let him go. I met with him all the time, and he does this to me? It isn't that I feel betrayed; it's not like that. It's that I just didn't see it coming. I thought we were all in this together.*

You've done everything right to sustain momentum. You focused on structural momentum and made sure everyone had the appropriate resources and responsibilities to get the job done. You focused on performance momentum, monitoring to assure that everyone knew what was expected of them and how they would be evaluated. You created cultural momentum by enhancing and sustaining everyone's motivation. In every way, you've shown yourself as a proactive leader who can stay on top of things and is managerially competent. You did not take your eye off the ball. Sometimes that is just not enough. Circumstances, conditions, situations change.

Sometimes challenges come out of nowhere. This is when you start to worry about political momentum.

Dale Martinez thought he was in cruising mode. He had spent the last eighteen months building support for the firm's controversial foray into the micro-finance sector, though it wasn't his idea. Raymond Chandler, his boss and mentor, had worked the idea at the board level. Martinez was the de facto leader of the initiative and the one who put his career—and his heart—on the line to make it happen.

Martinez had built a strong cadre of initial support. The initiative was a political minefield, as the power players in the organization were working multi-billion-dollar deals and saw micro-finance as a huge distraction for expensive talent without enough return on the "do-gooder" aspect of the activity. But Martinez was looking long-term and saw the core business at Generon Financial as drying up. Moreover, Generon just wasn't a big enough firm to get the biggest deals in the industry and needed some operating division that could deliver steady growth over the next two decades. Martinez was convinced that micro-finance was the ticket. And he was able to bring onboard some key executives in the firm and a strong group of allies in middle management and in lending operations.

After a year and a half of getting the business off the ground, Martinez felt like he had momentum. But a few unexpected events had put the continued growth of the micro-finance division at risk. First, Raymond Chandler had to leave the firm to care for his ailing wife. A few months after that, with the mergers and acquisitions unit showing record results, political upheaval in Colombia, one of Generon's key micro-finance markets, had triggered a red flag for the company's CFO and his risk managers. And Lester Schwam, one of Martinez's strongest allies and senior debt specialist, had accepted an offer to run the structured finance unit at one of the country's top banks.

In the course of a few months, the momentum Martinez had built was now seriously at risk. Martinez needed to bring on at least one other senior ally to replace the hole that Ray Chandler left. And he needed to plug some dissent within his group, as he tried to figure out a growth strategy that wasn't so heavily reliant on Colombia. Martinez felt like he was starting over from scratch. Deep down, he knew that wasn't the case. He had built a tremendous amount of political currency over the past eighteen months. And he still did have a strong base of support. But he was now missing some of the cover from others that he relied on to keep the project moving. And he felt that at any given time, Generon could shut down the initiative without looking back. After all, they built their business helping companies divest of nonperforming assets.

But how was Martinez going to keep the political momentum for his micro-finance unit alive and robust?

To succeed, Martinez cannot let his coalition slip away. He needs to stay in the coalition mindset. He has to figure out who is with him and who is against him. He has to figure out who is willing to do their bit and who is a free rider. He needs to anticipate splinter groups and countercoalitions.

In order to sustain momentum, you have to be politically smart—capable of anticipating conflict and opposition, while knowing who you're going to need on your side. If you want to successfully maintain momentum, you need to know how to deal with conflict and continuously mobilize support. Your capacity to manage political momentum will be the ultimate test of your ability to keep people on your side.

Those who attack the need for political skills are likely to maintain that as long as the initiative is a good one, as long as you're moving forward, you'll have no problem sustaining momentum, and certainly have no problem rallying people to your cause. The power of your idea and the honorable intent of your effort alone will assure you of continuous support. Is that really the case? In organizational settings, with shifting agendas, unstable turf, can you really be sure that those who are with you today will be in your corner tomorrow? Organizations are not temples of loyalty, where allegiance to ideas and individuals are primary. Organizational life is governed by rapidly changing opportunities. What is clearly to your benefit today, the best thing for your division to do right now, may be totally inappropriate and even harmful down the road. As your initiative moves down the road, it is critical that it is sustained by political momentum.

Don't Let the Coalition Mindset Slip Away

Shortly after the Challenger disaster, a safety coalition emerged at NASA. Hearings were held, resources were mobilized, new evaluation processes were put in place, and a collective safety culture emerged. There was a sense that something was getting done and that it would be sustained over time. This sense that something was going to get done came largely out of the vigorous sense of competency, purpose, and action that often comes with a coalition mindset. The problem arises when you move on down the road. Coalitions lose focus when alternatives emerge, outside pressures are exerted, and people become exhausted. That is what happened at NASA. As NASA was pressured to go back into the business of "flying the shuttle" and as memory faded, the safety coalition mindset slipped away. The coalition lost its focus and as a result, the Columbia met the same fate as the Challenger.

In sustaining political momentum, your challenge is not to let a coalition mindset drift away. In the simplest sense, a coalition is a collection of individuals or groups with common interests who are committed to the achievement of a common goal. A coalition is a group mobilized for joint action, with shared intentions and a shared understanding of what needs to be done. The key is the notion of mobilization. A coalition is formed not by accident or circumstance, but by the focused will of a managerially competent leader in order to mobilize others for joint action. As you move forward, your challenge is to sustain this feeling of mobilization and the sense that collectively, something of value can be achieved.

A coalition mindset is an energizing force. A group of individuals can work together at the same time, in the same office, and even on the same project. But if they don't share the sense that they are mobilized for a purpose and that they are moving together toward a specific end which they are all vested in, they are not a group capable of sustaining political momentum. Political momentum can only be sustained with a coalition mindset.

Think of a common criticism of the Democratic Party. While there are more registered Democrats than Republicans, there is a sense, real or not, that the Republicans operate, at its core, as a coalition with a focused agenda, common purposes, and with a sense of vision and mission. While there are internal differences, these differences seem to be contained beneath a common canopy. During the Reagan years, and early in the George W. Bush administration, there was a firm sense of this coalition mindset. To contrast, the Democrats, even under the Clinton administration, seemed to sprawl. While in the broadest sense they share a common political culture, they seem to be constantly torn asunder by an inability to articulate a common sense of purpose. Democrats are under a common canopy, but it is stretched so thin that every time it rains, everyone gets soaked.

A coalition mindset is critical to sustaining political momentum. In order to not lose the coalition mindset, you have to:

- Reinvigorate the vision
- Reinforce the benefits
- Sustain optimism
- Maintain your credibility

Reinvigorate the Vision

Sometimes sustaining momentum becomes drudgery. Day in and day out, feeling like Sisyphus, you roll the stone uphill hoping that it won't roll back on top of you. Sometimes it is the world of Willy Loman. Going to work, coming home, pushing ahead. You sit in your office plugging away at odds and ends and hope that something is moving. But at any given moment, it seems as if you are living on a glacier—going nowhere slowly. Even though it seems you made some progress, in reality, you are exactly where you were the day before.

In this context, what you need to do to sustain a coalition mindset is to reinvigorate the vision. A vision alone cannot sustain momentum. Managerially competent leaders know how to return to the vision periodically to remind people what the long-term objective is all about.

Let's return to Dale Martinez. Every six months, Martinez had a meeting of the members of his group, and once a year, he got on the docket to speak at the senior management retreat in Key West. In each of these meetings, Martinez went back to his original "slides" about why the firm was getting into micro-lending and the vision for the unit. Martinez used these opportunities to remind the organization why they were there. And it served as a strong introduction to people new to the firm.

One of the ways Martinez was able to sustain momentum was by appealing to the "do-good" nature of the micro-finance business. Yes, it was a profit-seeking enterprise. But being part of this initiative gave his high-powered financial staff a sense of making a difference. Martinez knew this wouldn't appeal to all the people in his organization. After all, most joined Generon to make large salaries and enormous bonuses. But there were still some very accomplished executives for whom the initiative held great appeal. And Martinez never failed to remind them of that.

The reinvigoration reminder re-engages people emotionally and re-establishes their sense of purpose and sense of vision. It refamiliarizes them with the very things that got them involved in the initiative originally, things they may have forgotten. To a certain degree, it is the charismatic, idealistic appeal. It is an effort to appeal to a sense of pride and to rally the troops.

Reinforce the Benefits

While charismatically reinforcing the vision is critical in sustaining the coalition mindset, there is also a need to revisit an individual's rational calculation. Sure, they joined your effort because they believed in it. But they also joined it because they expected certain benefits. Economists talk of the "expected utility" of belonging to a group. Just as when discussing motivation, people do ask, "What's in it for me?" In other words, people will decide whether to stay with your initiative on the basis of what rewards they are able to reap. It is rational to expect that they'll stay in a coalition mindset as long as they at least subjectively feel that the potential payoff of working with you versus working against you or on another initiative is beneficial to them.

Your responsibility in sustaining a coalition mindset is to make it clear to the critical sectors in the organization that what is essential to the bottom line is to put resources and time into your effort. It is important to reinvigorate vision, but it is equally important to remind everyone of the bottom-line payoff.

Martinez was asked to talk on a company-wide Web conference to present the status of the micro-finance initiative. "We are still on track to hit our numbers this quarter. But I want to reinforce how this initiative is supporting the long-term growth of the company. We believe that micro-finance can be a billion-dollar business if we do it right. If you see the chart, you'll note how our growth will start modestly but really take hold in 2008. But the financial benefit to the company isn't the only benefit we get. We are building tremendous support with the press, with governments overseas, and with grass-roots organizations around the country. Not only is the micro-finance business a long-term boon to the organization, it is already reaping short-term accolades from others in our industry."

Sustain Optimism

In keeping the coalition mindset, your capacity to sustain optimism is essential. You need to give people a sense that, sure, there are obstacles, sure, there are bumps on the road, sure, there are difficulties—but if you all hang together you can achieve success. A mistake that some leaders make is that they spin off into self-reflective negativism, thinking that if they share their hesitation and concern, they will create sympathetic alliances. They'll go to members of their group and tell them that they understand the difficulties and hope that the coalition mindset will be vitalized by mutual sympathy and a self-reflective downer. That's not likely to happen.

A better way to sustain the coalition mindset is with the simple statement, "Things are tough, yes. But, we're going to make it." When creating optimism you don't want to be naive. You want to make it clear that you understand what is holding you back, but that the obstacles and hurdles are surmountable. If you fail to project a sense of optimism, your coalition mindset will dissipate, no one will be on your side, and you're not going anyplace.

One of Dale Martinez's great strengths was his sense of calling and mission. He felt that success was within his reach. Martinez conveyed energy and a can-do attitude that permeated all his efforts. When he spoke, people felt that anything was possible. When people got around him, Martinez's sense of excitement and opportunity was contagious. Even though he spent many an evening sitting at his desk, eating Chinese take-out and worrying about the unit's financials, when it came time to meet with others in his unit, things only looked one way—up. And Martinez's ability to project that enthusiasm, confidence, and optimism was key in his ability to keep people engaged with the opportunity, even when things seemed dire.

Maintain Your Credibility

The coalition mindset is going to be sustained if people continue to believe in you and your ideas. Credibility implies that others have trust in your intent and in your capacity to stay with the program and move things forward. In order to sustain a coalition mindset, you need others to perceive that you have the credibility to push your initiative forward.[49] Remember that credibility is something that others confer on you; it's not something you solicit from them. Credibility may not guarantee others will agree with you, but it provides some assurance that they will give you the benefit of the doubt and stay with you. Without it, rest assured you're not moving forward.

When people initially get around your proposal, they are likely to view you as credible. As you move down the road and deal with the practical aspects of getting things done, your credibility may wear thin and questions may arise. Do you have the expertise to go the distance? Do you have the authority to make the important decisions? Do you really know what's going on? Do you have the personal integrity to stay the course and do the right thing?

Credibility is a quickly spent commodity. To assure that you sustain the coalition mindset, your credibility needs to be replenished from time to time.

Dale Martinez's credibility was partially based on his relationship with Ray Chandler. Because he worked so closely with the senior executive, he had the opportunity to see things in the firm and in the markets that were not apparent to many of his peers. That said, Martinez's own expertise and his experience at the World Bank and Credit Lyonnais gave everyone the sense that he understood development projects and the nuts and bolts of finance. But over the last year and a half, Martinez built on this foundation by delivering strong financial results and developing a reputation in the firm for being his own man. When Ray Chandler left, Martinez knew that this would be the real test of his credibility. It was through his consistently sound management decisions, dynamic personality, and impeccable integrity that Martinez was able to sustain momentum by leveraging his strong credibility with his staff.

Don't Feed the Trojan Horse

In sustaining political momentum, you may do everything possible to maintain the coalition mindset, trying to keep the group together and moving them forward in a collective direction. No matter what you do, it is inevitable that dissent will emerge. Not everyone will agree with everything that you do. It is likely that you will be challenged. As you know, it is important to sustain the collective, but not to dismiss the individual. If you stress the role of the individual, it is expected that dissent will emerge. Dissent and objections to your ideas, while uncomfortable, are not dysfunctional. Dissent can check groupthink in a positive way.[50]

Sometimes, you may overlook dissent by your need to sustain a coalition. You might not realize that the group that you started your initiative with may no longer be the group that you need now. To sustain momentum, you will need to revisit who is on your side, who you want to be on your side, and who you're willing to let go. Managers sometimes assume that the best thing they can do to push an initiative is to get as many people on their side as possible and keep them there. Having everyone in your group creates the potential of enabling the internal Trojan horse. Not every Trojan horse is brought in from outside of the walls of the project. Sometimes, a Trojan horse can be cobbled together by group members within the confines of your initiative. You may be able to predict the existence of an outside Trojan horse and take steps against lasting damage, but the internal Trojan horse presents its own special opportunity for sabotage. You need to be vigilant and diligent in sensing changing interests and intents of group members. And you need the courage to deal with internal opposition in a forthright and timely manner.

Sense Changing Interests

When your initiative begins, you're likely to feel strongly about the members of your team or group. You'll feel that they are in your corner. As things move along, the solidified group may splinter. Maybe your colleagues think you're being too conservative and want you to move at a faster pace. Some may feel your agenda is no longer relevant. Some may think you haven't given them the necessary resources. Others might maintain that your evaluation process is unfair. Still others may think the culture is too oppressive. Your challenge is to maintain a degree of cohesion and not let things spin out of control. You need to understand that not everyone who voices some discontent is out to destroy, sabotage, and scuttle your initiative. Discontent is not an obstacle to sustaining momentum. Managerially competent leaders have the capacity to differentiate *support*, *dissent*, *opposition*, and *resistance* among group members.

Supporters are those individuals who continue to agree with your agenda and how it is being executed. While they may raise questions about specifics, the general framework you are pursuing is more than acceptable to them. They feel the initiative is on the right track, and will have positive results.

Dissenters are those individuals who support your initiative but may question what you're doing and how you're going about doing it. Dissenters still share with you a common framework, but they want to make some adjustments as you're moving along.

Opponents, unlike dissenters, are likely to express stronger opposition about what you're doing and how you're getting there. While dissenters may make offhand remarks and suggestions, opponents are more likely to challenge you directly and publicly in an adamant and continuous fashion. Their language is more confrontational and reflects a stronger sense of urgency.

Resistors are those individuals who not only want to challenge you, but actively sabotage where you're going and how you're getting there. Resistors will verge on obstruction—not only confronting you, but also blocking you at every turn.

Generon's micro-finance unit quickly became a well-regarded presence in the industry. The fragmented industry had too many independent entrepreneurs who were conducting micro-lending operations. And the few large banks that entered the business did so more as a marketing tool for their standard, high-fee financial services. Generon was one of the early firms that had both size and commitment to the long-term growth of the industry segment. Dale Martinez was Generon's visible spokesperson for the unit and for the micro-lending business, generally. He spoke at major banking conferences, at public policy symposia, and at many nongovernmental organization events in lesser-developed countries. By the end of its first year of operations, you would think that Generon was one of the founders of micro-finance. Their name was everywhere in discussions about the sector and Martinez was very active in Washington lobbying efforts seeking favorable tax treatment for micro-lenders.

When Ray Chandler exited, Martinez faced his first leadership crisis and his first challenge to sustaining momentum for the unit. The question in most people's mind was not "Who will replace Chandler?" Most knew that it was unlikely that Generon would seek to replace Chandler, as Ray was too unique a talent and had a highly unstructured position at Generon. Most people were asking, "Can Martinez pull this off without Ray Chandler?"

Martinez would get a chance to provide some answers. In a forthcoming senior management meeting, Martinez was asked to present a status update on the micro-finance unit and a brief overview of the business's strategy for the next three years. Dale and Ray had been working on this presentation in different ways over the past three months. But the two hadn't come to a consensus position. There were several issues that were nagging at Dale, not least of which was the weakening of the dollar against local currencies in the countries that Generon's micro-lending activities were heaviest. But Dale hustled, got some of his confidants together, and they hammered out a strategy for the unit.

Dale knew that this meeting would be a dicey one. He knew there was a strong group of executives who did not care for him and who viewed micro-lending as something akin to the way a Las Vegas baccarat player would view a Saturday night bingo game at the local church. Whereas several of those executives had remained silent in the past, with Ray Chandler out of the picture, Dale felt that now was the time when the real dissenters would make their play against him.

Dale continued to believe that the firm's future would be rooted by micro-finance, in some way. Everything he read pointed in that direction and the enormous long-term global economic growth was projected to come from those countries whose GDP wasn't even a blip on an economist's radar. Prior to the meeting, Dale sat down with three other executives in his micro-lending group and began to assess the senior leadership and the likelihood of their support for his strategy.

James H. Brink, head of Asian mergers and acquisitions for Generon, seemed supportive of Martinez's agenda. His view was, "Asia continues to be the most critical for our future, and we need to have a unique presence in every country over there and at every level in each country's economy." Brink saw Martinez's initiative and the micro-finance activity, generally, as building the infrastructure of lesser-developed Asian countries and providing the long-term growth opportunities for Brink's mergers and acquisitions financing. Brink was not at all threatened by the micro-finance business and he and Martinez always had a very solid relationship together.

Martha Sonnenfeld had been with Generon for twelve years. Her expertise was domestic private equity investments. So, Martha didn't have much of a knowledge base in micro-finance. But she'd paid close attention to the discussions that had taken place in the past and she knew enough to be skeptical about the firm's entry into this market segment. And given that her business was the fastest growing segment in the company, she often wondered out loud in meetings, "Aren't we overemphasizing Asia, Africa, and South America? I mean, why place such a strong emphasis there, when the near-term growth opportunities in the United States are so high and coming from private equity investment?" But Martha also liked Dale and respected his intellect.

Maureen Foundling, a senior economist with the company, never quite got onboard with the micro-finance idea. Maureen had been with Generon for fifteen years and was deeply influential with the heads of the business units. Her forecasts had historically been quite accurate. Maureen had a very good relationship with Ray Chandler, but she was never afraid to challenge his positions. She was most concerned with the economic risks that the effort might create for the company. Her decision was based on balance of payments projections and her assessment of the dire economic trends in many of the countries where Generon's micro-lending activities took place. According to Foundling, "In concept, it is a provocative idea, but it is hard to justify putting a lot of money into South America, Pakistan, and Indonesia over the coming year."

Gunther Haverling headed the venture capital arm of Generon, specializing in international VC investment. Haverling was suspicious of Martinez, and had been ever since Dale joined the firm. And he was an outspoken critic of Ray Chandler, too. Haverling felt that Martinez was using the micro-finance "vision" as a way of making an end run at Haverling's venture capital business. Haverling couldn't understand why Martinez would want to go into the micro-business, when the stakes and payouts were so much higher in the VC business. Haverling's only explanation was that Martinez was using it as an entry into the VC market. "I simply don't understand nor agree with how this fits into our strategy. These investments are too small, insignificant, and are not worth the paper they are printed on. We are in the business of making big bucks on big investments. This is like having Cartier start selling Swatch watches. If we push Dale's agenda, we really run the risk of watering down our brand and weakening our position in markets overseas. We have to remain a boutique investment house for high-growth businesses all over the world."

Martinez looks at the senior managers, and what does he see? Clearly, James Brink is a supporter who understands and is committed to Martinez's vision. Martha Sonnenfeld is a dissenter. She has some conflicting opinions—wanting to slow Generon's expansion overseas. Even though she is a dissenter on particular points, she is not an active opponent. Maureen Foundling is an active opponent. Foundling is deeply concerned about the economic risk that the initiative may pose for the company, even though she doesn't oppose the idea of micro-finance, per se. Gunther Haverling is going to be a resistor all the way. He thinks micro-lending is entirely the wrong strategy for Generon and he feels threatened by Dale's effort. There is no way he will support this initiative. Martinez's challenge is to obtain enough senior leadership support so that his micro-finance initiative can be sustained. But Dale needs to do so in such a way that he will not create splinter groups. The last thing in the world you want to do when facing opposition to your initiative is to create splinter groups.

Deal with Internal Opposition

You've identified the position of the key actors. Whatever you do, don't react too quickly and don't overreact. This may seem self-evident, but it is a truth that is often ignored. Your reaction to internal criticism will vary from being mildly defensive to feeling betrayed. There is a tendency to jump down people's throats at the earliest available opportunity. This is one sure way of destroying political momentum.

A misstep that some inexperienced leaders make is to squelch internal criticism. They view criticism as divisive and as a threat to their ability to lead the effort. They view their leadership in an authoritative way and take measures and develop systems that try to prevent criticism from coming to a public forum. In their pursuit of a controlled, methodical initiative, they keep all dissent bottled up. Although sometimes this strategy succeeds, more often than not, it is a recipe for disaster. It can create so much pent-up frustration that very quickly, the group leader can find herself with a mutiny on her hands.

Managerially competent leaders understand that they need to select a time and a place to respond to criticism, and they know not to overreact. Any reaction you make is public. Once the genie is out of the bottle, there is no way of getting it back in. Once you are seen as having a paranoid overreaction, you will damage your credibility and the credibility of your initiative. The danger is that you have already slipped into a conflict spiral.

The project was going along pretty well and I thought I'd check with Rick about the possibility of converting the online processes to face-to-face sales in the Omaha area. Boy, did he go berserk.

He got defensive. I know he is behind online sales, but I was just thinking, in Omaha, we have enough people on the ground. Makes you wonder why he's so uptight. I thought I understood his agenda, but maybe I'm missing something here.

The conflict spiral has now begun as a result of Rick's overreaction.

In dealing with internal challenges the choice is between hard or soft tactics. You need to choose between tactics of coercion and tactics of persuasion. Hard tactics rely on the use of threats and confrontation. Hard tactics are embedded in your authority to call the shots and are often used as an ultimatum. The goal of confrontational tactics is to call people to task, and the blatant consequences may be to drive them out. Soft tactics rely on promises and co-optation. Soft tactics are embedded in your own personal capacity to influence people. The goal of persuasive tactics is to incorporate people and keep them on your side.

In sustaining political momentum, your challenge is to know when to use which tactic. A directive leader may be inclined to use hard tactics, while a facilitative leader may be predisposed to soft tactics. A managerially competent leader knows when to use which tactic for which situation. When facing supporters, obviously, this is a nonissue. They are already on your side. You'll be exchanging ideas freely all the time.

When dealing with dissenters, you will also want to use soft tactics. You already know they are inclined to go with your agenda—they just would prefer some modification. Dissenters are reaching out to you for a little flexibility. Some persuasion and a bit of concession will go a long way.

Opponents present a problem. You want them on your side, but they're sitting on the fence. Over time, they voice more and more criticism as to how things operate. They are not locked against you, but they have reservations whether they can work with you and your agenda. You want to begin with soft tactics with opponents. You want to give them a sense that they are being listened to, but you have to balance your facilitative inclination to use soft tactics with your directive inclination. Dialogue, persuasion, and the use of soft tactics can go on endlessly. While soft tactics give efficacy and confidence to opponents that their input counts, you also have to bind the discussion with a sense of authority. You have to let them know that you intend to move your agenda forward and that there is a limit to dialogue and facilitation. You want to make it clear to them that nondecisions are not acceptable and that you'll be willing to make the hard decisions when the time comes. With opponents, you want to speak softly, but carry a big stick.

If you use soft tactics with resistors, they will prolong the discussions and showcase the negotiations. They will use this airing of differences as a way to get dissenters and opponents on their side. They will very happily do whatever they can to derail your momentum. In light of the damage that resistors can wreck on your initiative, you need to make a hard leadership decision—you have to decide if you're willing to let them go. In dealing with resistors, you need to understand that *you don't need everyone on your side to sustain momentum.*

Martinez had to make up his mind and decide whom he needed on his side—and who was not worth the effort. He didn't need to spend time with James Brink, the head of mergers and acquisitions. Brink was clearly on Martinez's side and was already publicly supporting him.

Martinez could spend some time with Martha Sonnenfeld to make sure that she doesn't become a member of a splinter group. All he had to do was convince her, using soft tactics, that he wasn't overemphasizing Asia, Africa, and South America and that in the future he would give more emphasis to growth opportunity in the United States. With a little discussion, a little persuasion, and a little facilitation, she would be strongly in his corner.

Maureen Foundling required both soft and hard tactics. While she was a potential ally, she had some major reservations. Martinez would have to devote a lot of time to sitting with her, going over the numbers, and discussing the issues. Finally, he knew that both of them would have to fish or cut bait, otherwise the dialogue would go on forever. Martinez's hope was to get Maureen to go along with him, James, and Martha in a common effort.

As for Gunther, there was no hope. All the facilitation in the world would go nowhere. If Martinez wasn't careful, Gunther could reach out to Maureen and form a countercoalition. That was his worst nightmare. There was no way around it. No soft tactics here. With Gunther, it would be hard tactics all the way. The best thing he could do would be to push him off the stage as soon as possible.

Beware of Countercoalitions

You may have done all you can to keep the coalition in place and to sustain political momentum. You may have done your best to avoid the Trojan horse. But countercoalitions will emerge. This is part of organizational life: You move an initiative, and sooner or later, a countercoalition will come to the fore.

You need to understand the difference between countercoalitions and other groups, such as interest groups and splinter groups, which may challenge you. Organizations are naturally comprised of interest groups—collections of individuals whose interests at any point are not consistent with yours. For the most part, interest groups are passive and don't actively seek to change the direction or mobilize against your effort. They may try to sway you, but they will be relatively passive about it. Most significantly, interest groups don't act collectively—they don't have a sense of a collective interest. A splinter group acts more strongly than an interest group. A splinter group understands two things: they aren't happy with what you're doing and they want to make modest efforts to change the direction of where the organization is headed. Unlike interest groups, splinter groups realize the potential for collective action. They'll meet with you as a group, but they are reluctant to push the issue too far. Both of these are easier to deal with than a full-fledged countercoalition. A countercoalition is a group of politically active individuals who disagree with your agenda and will publicly challenge it. They are aware of their common interests as a group. They are collectively aware that they are in direct opposition of where you want to go.[51]

Your challenge is to make sure that splinter groups don't become countercoalitions—and that you recognize the challenge that countercoalitions can pose to your momentum. To sustain momentum, you need to be aware when these groups develop and the underlying agendas upon which they are built. Too many group leaders ignore the existence of countercoalitions, only to find that their initiative was derailed by a group of people who felt threatened by the effort or who felt there was a better solution to a particular organizational problem. Many managers operate with political blinders on.

By not recognizing the existence of countercoalitions, leaders run the risk of losing the commitment and support from their core constituents. Group members are rarely comfortable with a leader who is operating like an ostrich with his head in the sand while the group members feel the resistance first- or secondhand. Also, by not recognizing countercoalitions that inevitably exist, a leader can lull her group into complacency and irrelevance over time, thereby losing the critical mass that is so important to keeping an idea moving. This is at the heart of building political momentum.

Dale Martinez has to manage his effort very carefully. Gunther Haverling and, to a lesser degree, Maureen

Foundling have the potential to create a countercoalition to derail Martinez's effort. Martinez's interaction with Haverling has not been positive and he is running the risk of inciting Haverling to action. Even if Martinez doesn't want that to happen, Haverling may feel threatened enough to take action against Martinez. But he needs to stay keenly aware.

In the best situation, Haverling and Foundling may form an interest or splinter group. They may serve as watchdogs—ensuring that the micro-finance unit stays on course and does not overconsume organization resources nor put the company at undue risk. They may remain pure critics of the initiative, keeping Martinez on the defensive and, perhaps, negotiating for resources for their own efforts. In this case, Martinez may find it more difficult to move things forward and maintain momentum, but he will be need to be less concerned about others actually derailing his efforts.

Martinez needs to manage his relationships with Haverling and Foundling carefully. On the one hand, he does not want to incite them to activism. He doesn't, nor does any other leader, want a countercoalition to develop. They are draining to deal with. So, Martinez may be willing to give up a few things here or there—negotiate for certain resources, promise to stay clear of specific lightning rods—all in the pursuit of avoiding a countercoalition. But Martinez needs to be careful not to go too far. It is easy to become a slave to the threat of a countercoalition. If Martinez gives in too much, yields on too many issues, he is likely to hamper his effort on his own. He needs to stay tough and maintain his position, while knowing when to give in. It is clearly more art than science. But it is an important art for all leaders to develop if they are to sustain momentum over the long term.

Leaders who keep people on their side are those who recognize and pay attention to resistance, countercoalitions, and splinter groups, to a point. These leaders keep their antennas out and active, staying fully aware of the camps of opposition in the organization. They go a step further to make their own group aware of the different camps of resistance and the arguments those opposing groups are making against their initiative. The very best leaders are careful about not obsessing over the opposition.

Overreacting to countercoalitions can be as damaging as ignoring their very existence. Leaders who are unable to maintain the momentum of their initiatives and the commitment of their members often overreact or raise unnecessary awareness of other groups of detractors. By paying too much attention to sources of opposition, you may in fact give those groups a legitimacy that they would not have had if you simply recognized their existence but did little else to respond to their arguments. Once you respond to an opposing point of view, you, in effect, validate that point of view.

Emphatic responses to a countercoalition or splinter group can also detract from the momentum of your group. Once you begin paying too much attention to an opposition group, your group runs the risk of losing its direction and its critical mass. People in your group begin to take your cues and spend more of their time responding to the countercoalition than they do pursuing the group's agenda. And in some extreme cases, the countercoalition's argument can start making good sense to your group's members, to the point that they lose commitment to your initiative and begin to support the opposing point of view.

Directive leaders may run the risk of dismissing dissent and opposition too quickly, because their focus may be so narrow that they can't respond to legitimate criticism appropriately. Facilitative leaders may run the risk of trying to incorporate everybody and mistakenly accommodate dissenters who are not respected or who have unfounded criticism. If you make the mistake of including everyone, you may destroy your credibility among the high-powered players who've already bought in or who are on the fence. Managerially competent leaders try to distinguish real dissent versus white noise. Giving too much weight to ad-hoc opposition or not giving enough attention to a serious criticism can ruin your credibility.

So, finding the balance where you remain aware of the existence of countercoalitions and respond to their position in an appropriate and measured way (or, not at all, as necessary) is something that successful leaders do to keep people on their side and to maintain the momentum of their initiative. They do not go so far as to be overly responsive to criticism and opposition, nor do they shift the other way and become ignorant of the very existence of countercoalitions. It is a delicate balance, but the stuff that real political momentum and leadership success is made of.

Chapter 8

The Proactive Leader:
Get Them and Keep Them on Your Side

> *You know, these people have called more meetings than Congress. Every other day, a different meeting to discuss this, discuss that. In Omaha, if my boss had an idea, it was get out of the way, full steam ahead. No consulting, no nothing. A few token gestures, maybe, but that was it. He didn't get it either. Don't these people understand that you have to do a little of this, a little of that. You want to get people in your corner and you want to get something done. It doesn't mean that we need to retreat on the third-floor conference room all the time. But, we don't want to be in Omaha either, where you have to get out of the way.*

Some leaders are able to get people on their side. But they falter when it comes to moving their agenda forward. This is, perhaps, the most common scenario that leaders face. The result? A perhaps well-liked leader who is deemed ineffective. Or, one with a good idea that was poorly executed. The corporate and nonprofit world is littered with examples of leaders who fall into this category. They are known as *obsessive consensus builders*.[52] They get people on their side and work tirelessly to maintain their support, even at the expense of showing results. They tend to take consensus building to an extreme.

Consensus builders seem to operate with the assumption that if they can get people to support their effort, those people will mobilize and push through their agenda, without a great deal of effort on the part of the leader. Unfortunately for obsessive consensus builders, this reasoning is deeply flawed in 99 percent of organizations.

You've seen obsessive consensus builders in action. They are the ones who call a lot of meetings. They spend a lot of time visiting the offices of colleagues or calling them on the phone. They are consumed with ensuring that their coalition members are onboard with their effort. These consensus builders are obsessed with unity around big issues such as mission, purpose, and strategy, and they end up getting bogged down with unnecessary minutiae. Their meetings seem to be a series of contradictions. They try to rally everyone around their common sense of calling and rely on superficial humanistic clichés. They're great with eye contact and process. At the same time, they exercise micromanagement, making sure that everyone and everything is moving in the same direction. Often, obsessive consensus builders are unable or uninterested in showing results. Sometimes it is simply a matter of time—they spend all their time keeping people on their side, so they don't have enough time to get things done.

Sometimes leaders never really get people on their side. These are the *lone rangers*. They are so fixated with getting things done that they try to get everyone out of their way unless they are immediately necessary. They are results-driven, believing that "action speaks louder than words." Some lone rangers are the drill sergeants who relentlessly drive people to perform the tasks that need to get done. Other lone rangers quietly pursue their agenda, preferring to do the work themselves and occasionally giving others certain isolated tasks. Regardless of how they do it, lone rangers see the end clearly and remain uniquely focused on getting there.

Because they don't spend enough time getting people on their side, lone rangers often create divisions within their organizations. The organization may make progress toward the leader's desired goals, but no one has a sense of ownership over the process or the results. Those who survive the charge of the lone ranger are relieved that they weren't trampled.

Proactive leaders incorporate the best qualities of consensus builders and lone rangers. Like consensus builders, proactive leaders know it is critical to mobilize support. Like lone rangers, proactive leaders know it is essential to achieve results. Proactive leaders understand that support feeds results, and results feed support. Proactive leaders understand the importance of political competence and managerial competence. They understand that they need political competence to get people on their side to rally around their agenda, and managerial competence to sustain momentum and keep people on their side.

The premise of *Get Them on Your Side* is that there are three critical skills you need to develop in order to get people on your side. First, you need to map the political terrain. You need to understand who are your allies and resistors, antici-pate their reaction, and analyze their agendas. Second, you need to get them on your side by getting initial support by justifying your action, and creating an agenda. Third, you need to make things happen. You do this by getting people to buy in to your ideas and put your ideas in place. Your political competence is measured by your ability to map the political terrain, get them on your side, and make things happen.

POLITICAL COMPETENCE

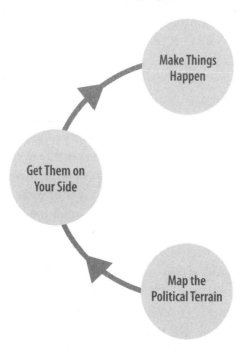

Proactive leaders do more than get people on their side. They implement, execute, and see ideas to fruition. Proactive leaders start initiatives, sustain them, and complete them. They do more than rally everyone around them. They do more than create coalitions. They do more than legitimize their agenda. They put their agenda in place. Proactive leaders know how to sustain momentum and not just get people on their side, but keep them there. Proactive leaders know how to deal with the day-in, day-out, nuts-and-bolts questions that arise when agendas are pushed in organizations. Proactive leaders are not simply politically competent; they are also managerially competent.

This volume presents the basic skills you need to sustain momentum, keep people on your side, and prove your managerial competence. First, different conditions demand different leadership responses. A key to your managerial competence is your capacity to know when to respond in a directive fashion and when to respond in a facilitative style. At one point a facilitative response may be most appropriate to sustain momentum, while at others, a directive response may be more important. In sustaining momentum, you must walk the tightrope between directive and facilitative leadership.

This is not enough. You also have to understand that momentum is not simply an idea, but a phenomenon that can be controlled. This book introduces eleven principles of managerial competence that will help you sustain momentum.

Managerial Competence

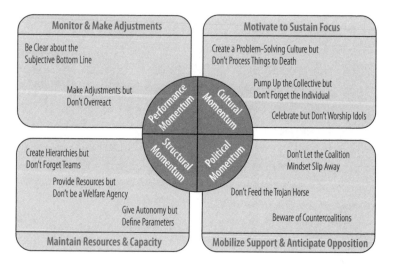

Monitor & Make Adjustments	Motivate to Sustain Focus
Be Clear about the Subjective Bottom Line	Create a Problem-Solving Culture but Don't Process Things to Death
Make Adjustments but Don't Overreact	Pump Up the Collective but Don't Forget the Individual
	Celebrate but Don't Worship Idols

Performance Momentum   Cultural Momentum   Structural Momentum   Political Momentum

Create Hierarchies but Don't Forget Teams	Don't Let the Coalition Mindset Slip Away
Provide Resources but Don't be a Welfare Agency	
Give Autonomy but Define Parameters	Don't Feed the Trojan Horse
	Beware of Countercoalitions
Maintain Resources & Capacity	**Mobilize Support & Anticipate Opposition**

Structural momentum: In maintaining resources and capacity to enhance structural momentum, you want to make sure the organizational structures are consistent with what you're trying to achieve. If you don't give people the right resources and enough autonomy and if you create too many hierarchies, your initiative will come to a halt. You need to give people the resources that they need, but you have to be careful that you don't become that welfare agency that responds to every request. Give them autonomy, but know when to pull in the reins. Create hierarchies, but respect teams. Balance your directive inclination to control through hierarchy, specify parameters, and be tight with resources with your facilitative tendency to use teams, give autonomy, and be generous with resources. Remember, it's a balancing act.

Performance momentum: In dealing with performance momentum you want to monitor performance and make adjustments. In monitoring performance, you have to know what you're monitoring and what you're going to be evaluating. You can't just make evaluations willy-nilly and think that you won't slow down your initiative. You also have to make adjustments. In doing so, you can't overreact. Don't let yourself be sidetracked by every new idea and every criticism.

Cultural momentum: You want to motivate with cultural momentum to keep everyone focused on your initiative. You want to do this by creating a problem-solving culture that doesn't get stuck in perpetual procrastination. You want to give people the sense they're part of a collective, without making them cultural automatons. Finally, you want to use rituals and ceremonies to give recognition, but you don't want them to become ends in their own right. You want to celebrate accomplishment, but not worship idols. You want to create a collective culture of motivation, but not stifle individual creativity by supporting groupthink.

Political momentum: You want to mobilize support and anticipate opposition with political momentum. You'll achieve this by sustaining a coalition mindset. A coalition mindset gives people the sense they share a common purpose. Don't let this mindset slip away. You'll also sustain political momentum by understanding who are your internal supporters, dissenters, opponents, and resistors. If you don't do this, you may create a Trojan horse, which could be the downfall of your agenda. You want to be vigilant and aware of countercoalitions, which can always emerge. Lastly, don't cross the line between cautious politics and neurotic paranoia.

Keep these principles in mind and you'll be able to sustain momentum and keep people on your side. Combine these with the principles presented in *Get Them on Your Side*, and you will become a truly proactive leader and people will say . . .

He's a leader who can mobilize people around his ideas, knows how to sustain momentum, keep people on his side, and go the distance!

Relevant Reading

Ambrose, Stephen. *Undaunted Courage* (New York: Simon and Schuster, 1997).

Bacharach, Samuel B. *Get Them on Your Side* (Avon, MA: Platinum Press, 2005).

Bacharach, Samuel B., and Edward J. Lawler. *Power and Politics* (San Francisco: Jossey-Bass, 1980).

Bossidy, Larry, and Ram Charan. *Execution: The Discipline of Getting Things Done* (New York: Crown Business, 2002).

Brock, Timothy C., and Melanie C. Green, eds. *Persuasion: Psychological Insights and Perspectives,* 2nd edition (Thousand Oaks, CA: Sage, 2005).

Brooks, Frederick P. *The Mythical Man-Month: Essays on Software Engineering,* 20th Anniversary Edition (Reading, MA: Addison-Wesley Professional, 1995).

Etzioni, Amitai. *A Comparative Analysis of Complex Organizations* (New York: Free Press, 1975).

Galbraith, Jay. *Designing Complex Organizations: An Execution Guide to Strategy, Structure, and Process* (Reading, MA: Addison-Wesley, 1973).

Goodwin, Doris Kearns. *Team of Rivals: The Political Genius of Abraham Lincoln* (New York: Simon and Schuster, 2005).

Hackman, Richard, and Greg Oldham. *Work Redesign* (Reading, MA: Addison Wesley, 1999).

Hechter, Michael. *Principles of Group Solidarity* (Berkeley: University of California Press, 1987).

Janis, Irving. *Groupthink* (Boston, MA: Houghton-Mifflin, 1982).

Kouzes, James M., and Barry Z. Posner. *Credibility: How Leaders Gain and Lose It, Why People Demand It* (San Francisco: Jossey-Bass, 2003).

Kunda, Gideon. *Engineering Culture: Control and Commitment in a High-Tech Corporation* (Philadelphia, PA: Temple University Press, 1993).

Martin, Joanne. *Organizational Culture: Mapping the Terrain* (Thousand Oaks, CA: Sage, 2002).

McGregor, Douglas. *The Human Side of Enterprise* (New York: Prentice Hall, 1960).

Ostroff, Frank. *The Horizontal Organization* (New York: Oxford University Press, 1999).

Pressman, Jeffrey L., and Aaron Wildavsky. *Implementation*, 3rd edition (Berkeley: University of California Press, 1984).

Schein, Edgar H. *Organizational Culture and Leadership*, 2nd edition (San Francisco: Jossey-Bass, 1992).

Schon, Donald. *The Reflective Practitioner: How Professionals Think in Action* (New York: Basic Books, 1983).

Sonnenstuhl, William. *Working Sober: The Transformation of an Occupational Drinking Culture* (Ithaca, NY: ILR Press, 1996).

Trice, Harrison, and Janice Beyer, *The Cultures of Work Organizations* (Englewood Cliffs, NJ: Prentice Hall, 1993).

Endnotes

Chapter One

1. Recently, Larry Bossidy and Ram Charan (*Execution*, Crown Business, 2002) have popularized the notion of execution. However, in the context of this book, execution is not simply a rallying cry for action, but a specific set of skills that leaders and managers use to put ideas in place. I believe these skills are centered on the managerial challenges of mobilization and sustaining momentum.

2. In *Get Them on Your Side* (Platinum Press, 2005), I elaborate these as the primary skills necessary to establish your political competence.

3. Not placing enough emphasis on analyzing the agendas and understanding the interests of others is a primary mistake that managers make. The challenge for any politically competent manager is to begin implementing an initiative by understanding the relationship between

her agenda and the agenda of others (*Get Them on Your Side*, Platinum Press, 2005).

4. "Carly v. Walter," *The Economist*, 26 January 2002.

5. "Former Girl Scouts Chief Teams up with 'Father of Modern Management to Teach Leadership Skills,'" *The NonProfit Times*, December 1990.

6. Ann I. Mahoney and Gerry Romano, "Exploring Our Toughest Questions," *Association Management* 6, no. 49 (1997).

7. Frances Hesselbein, *Hesselbein on Leadership* (San Francisco: Jossey-Bass, 2004).

8. Ibid.

Chapter Two

9. Samuel Bacharach and Peter Bamberger, "Beyond Situational Constraints: Job Resources Inadequacy and Individual Performance at Work," *Human Resource Management Review*, 1995, p. 84. This paper attempts to show how resources are often ignored and the primary argument is that you can motivate people, but if you can't give them the resources to get the job done, good luck.

10. Ibid., p. 85.

11. Doris Kearns Goodwin, *Team of Rivals: The Political Genius of Abraham Lincoln* (New York: Simon and Schuster, 2005), p. 383. This book offers one of the best studies of how leaders sustain the momentum of their initiative. It presents Lincoln as an organizational manager, *par excellence*. The insights of the Lincoln discussion are drawn from this book.

12. Some of the best and most accessible work in this area has been done by Jay Galbraith (*Designing Complex Organizations*, Addison-Wesley, 1973) who makes it clear that organizational design issues are strategic choices available to managers. Another volume of interest is Frank Ostroff's *The Horizontal Organization* (New York: Oxford University Press, 1999).

13. J. Richard Hackman and Greg R. Oldham, *Work Redesign* (Reading, MA: Addison-Wesley, 1999). Hackman's work on job design is essential reading for any organizational manager who deals with critical issues such as how to design a job appropriately so that the work is executed and is consistent with expectations. Hackman's work is truly a classic in organizational theory.

14. James Wynbrandt, *Flying High* (Hoboken, NJ: Wiley, 2004).

15. Judith Glaser, *Creating We* (Avon, MA: Platinum Press, 2005).

16. Samuel Bacharach, *On The Front Line: The Work of First Responders in a Post 9/11 World* (Ithaca, NY: Cornell ILR, 2004). This two-year study necessitated working closely with hundreds of New York City firefighters after 9/11. One of the things I took away from this study was their belief that momentum could be sustained in even the worst situations over long periods of time. The key to the sustainability is a culture that creates focused drive.

17. Goodwin, p. 565.

18. "Looking Beyond the Mouse," *The Economist*, 28 January 2006.

Chapter Three

19. Douglas McGregor, *The Human Side of Enterprise* (New York: Prentice Hall, 1960). McGregor called this "Theory X" and "Theory Y." This distinction dominates many of the dichotomies of management theory. It differentiates between two different approaches to management theory.

20. John Horton, "The Dehumanization of Anomie and Alienation: A Problem in the Ideology of Sociology,"

The British Journal of Sociology, 1964, pp. 283–300. The classic distinction between anomie and alienation is often ignored, but critical to managers in organizations. Anomie is a concept often associated with the work of Emil Durkheim, the nineteenth-century French sociologist, and deals with the lack of norms and the lack of rules and regulations. Those managers who believe the primary problem in the workplace is anomie are inclined to increase the number of rules and regulations. The opposite is the alienation problem, associated with the work of Karl Marx. This framework maintains that managers concerned with alienation think that too many rules lead to stagnation and dehumanization. To compensate, the managers concerned with alienation have a tendency to want to use the minimum amount of rules and regulations. To put it simply, one group thinks that momentum is killed by too few rules; and the other thinks that momentum is killed by too many rules.

21. This notion of reflection in the workplace is best expressed by Donald Schon in *The Reflective Practitioner* (New York: Basic Books, 1983). Enhancing reflective action is the main goal of facilitative leadership. Assuring a nonreflective, or reflexive, action is the main goal of directive leadership.

22. This example was provided by James Biolos, management consultant.

23. This section on Lewis and Clark has greatly relied on the work conducted by Shane Messner. Certain paragraphs come directly from his paper (*Lewis and Clark: The Corps of Discovery*) that he submitted as a requirement of my undergraduate seminar. I'm very appreciative of his work and contribution to this book, as well as his generosity.

24. Letter to Dr. Benjamin Smith Barton, 27 February 1803, in *The Writings of Thomas Jefferson*, ed. H. A. Washingon (New York: H.W. Derby, 1861); available at *http:// yamaguchy.netfirms.com.*

25. Jack Uldrich, "Leading into the Unknown: How Lewis and Clark Built a Great Team," *Leader to Leader,* 2004; available at *www.pfdf.org.*

26. Stephen Ambrose, *Undaunted Courage* (New York: Simon and Schuster, 1997).

27. Ibid.

Chapter Four

28. It should be noted that the distinction between hierarchies and teams does not imply a mutually exclusive choice, but rather tactical alternatives that have to be considered in the context of a specific situation.

29. Frederick P. Brooks, *The Mythical Man-Month: Essays on Software Engineering*, 20th Anniversary Edition (Reading, MA: Addison-Wesley Professional, 1995).

Chapter Five

30. Social psychologists have identified this issue as the "attribution of causality" problem. When it's not clear how and why you attribute cause to a phenomenon, the ambiguity of cause and effect will be problematic. In an organizational setting, this ambiguity regarding cause and effect will not only be problematic, but it can also create the kind of anxiety and hesitation that can curtail momentum.

31. In their classic study of policy implementation (*Implementation*, University of California Press, 1974) Pressman and Wildavsky point out that one of the major gaps in adjusting policy is evaluation and utilization of performance data: "Swimming in a sea of complexity, evaluators begin to wonder if it is all worthwhile: Why should they struggle so hard to produce [data] about programs and policy if no one is going to use it?" (p. 198).

32. Peters and Waterman, *In Search of Excellence* (New York: Harper and Row, 1982). Peters and Waterman develop the concept of "managing by wandering around," showing

how some of the most effective organizations use this
style of communication to monitor and give feedback.

Chapter Six

33. E. Deci, R. Koestner, and R. Ryan, "A Meta-analytic
Review of Experiments Examining the Effects of Extrinsic
Rewards on Intrinsic Motivation," *Psychological Bulletin*,
1999. Roland Benabou and Jean Tirole, "Intrinsic and
Extrinsic Motivation," *Review of Economic Studies*, 2003.

34. Amitai Etzioni, *A Comparative Analysis of Complex Organizations* (New York: Free Press, 1975).

35. John Battelle, "Turning the Page," *CNN Money*, 1 July
2005. Quoting Anne Mulcahy, CEO, Xerox.

36. Keith H. Hammonds, "The Not-So-Quick Fix," *Fast
Company*, 2005. Interview with Anne M. Mulcahy.

37. The discussion of culture has been dominated by anthro-
pologists such as Clyde Kluckhohn, A. R. Radcliffe-
Brown, E. E. Evans-Pritchard, and Clifford Geertz. In the
last twenty years, culture has entered the field of management and organizational behavior. For a detailed discussion of culture and organizations, see Joanne Martin,
Organizational Culture (Thousand Oaks, CA: Sage, 2002);

also see Harrison Trice and Janice Beyer, *The Cultures of Work Organizations* (Englewood Cliffs, NJ: Prentice Hall, 1993). This is the most comprehensive text on the theory of organizational culture to date. Detailed and insightful, it offers an analytical, intellectual, and practical approach to organizational culture.

38. Peters and Waterman, *In Search of Excellence*.

39. Schon, *The Reflective Practitioner*.

40. Peter Bamberger, Dana Vashdi, and Mia Erez, "Briefing-Debriefing: Using a reflexive organizational learning model from the military to enhance the performance of surgical teams." Working paper.

41. Samuel B. Bacharach, *Get Them on Your Side* (Avon, MA: Platinum Press, 2005).

42. Herbert Simon, "Theories of Bounded Rationality," in McGuire and Radner, eds., *Decision and Organization* (North Holland: Amsterdam, 1972). Simon's notion of bounded rationality is critical to understand decisions under conditions of uncertainty, under pressure of time, and restriction of resources.

43. Irving Janis, *Groupthink* (Boston, MA: Houghton-Mifflin, 1982).

44. Mary F. Rousseau, *Community: The Tie That Binds* (Lanham, MD: University Press of America, 1991).

45. William Sonnenstuhl, *Working Sober* (Ithaca, NY: ILR Press, 1996). This is a fascinating study of the difficulties in changing culture and the role of rituals and ceremonies in the workplace.

46. Samuel Bacharach and William Sonnenstuhl, *The Forgotten American Worker*, manuscript.

47. "Ford's Whizzes Get 'Pulitzers,'" *Ward's Auto World*, January 1994.

48. For an interesting study of how culture can backfire when used strictly as a control device, see Gideon Kunda's *Engineering Culture* (Philadelphia, PA: Temple University Press, 1993).

Chapter Seven

49. Bacharach, *Get Them on Your Side*, and James M. Kouzes and Barry Z. Posner, *Credibility* (San Francisco: Jossey-Bass, 2003.

50. Charlan Jeanne Nemeth and Jack A. Goncalo, "Influence and Persuasion in Small Groups," in Timothy C.

Brock and Melanie C. Green, eds., *Persuasion*, 2nd edition (Thousand Oaks, CA: Sage, 2005).

51. Samuel B. Bacharach and Edward J. Lawler, *Power and Politics* (San Francisco: Jossey-Bass, 1980).

Chapter Eight

52. Bacharach, *Get Them on Your Side*. Keep in mind that it's important to draw a distinction between obsessive consensus builders and move consensus builders. Consensus building has a real role in the proactive process. Obsessive consensus builders see consensus building as an end in its own right. Consensus builders who are proactive leaders see consensus building as part of a process.

Index

About the Author

SAMUEL B. BACHARACH is the McKelvey-Grant Professor in the Department of Organizational Behavior at the School of Industrial and Labor Relations at Cornell University. He is the director of Cornell's New York City-based Institute for Workplace Studies and the Smithers Institute. He is the author and editor of over twenty books on management, organizational behavior, and industrial relations. His research has been published in most of the major academic journals.

Get Them on Your Side: Win Support, Convince Skeptics, and Get Results (Platinum Press, 2005) and now *Keep Them on Your Side: Leading and Managing for Momentum* are Professor Bacharach's effort to translate his thirty years of academic research on negotiation, organizational behavior, industrial relations, and leadership into books that are practical and accessible to practitioners. Both books address the theme of proactive leadership. *Get Them on Your Side* focuses on the skills of political competence, how to create coalitions, and how to mobilize people around good ideas. *Keep Them on Your Side* highlights managerial competence and the skills needed to sustain momentum.

Professor Bacharach teaches the discipline of proactive leadership to executives, politicians, managers, and students around the world. Besides teaching these concepts in depth to undergraduate and graduate students at Cornell's School of Industrial and Labor Relations, he develops and runs workshops and engages in individual coaching through the Kaaterskill Group (www.kaaterskillgroup .com). His workshops and seminars have been used by many organizations, such as Chubb Insurance, E*trade, Tiffany, Pepsi Americas, Starwood Hotels and Resorts, YMCA, and Borders Inc. His courses are also offered through Cornell's ILR Management Program and online through eCornell.

He lives in downtown Manhattan with his wife and son, where he also spends time dabbling in art criticism and novel writing.

To learn more about Professor Bacharach, the concepts in his books, and the courses offered, visit *www.getthemonyourside.com* and *www.keepthemonyourside.com*.

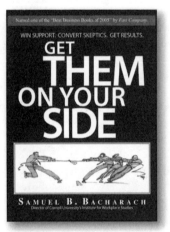